Skiing!

Faceplants, Eggbeaters and Snowsnakes:

A Guide to the Ski Bum Lifestyle

by
Carol Poster

Illustrated by Calvin Grondahl

ICS BOOKS, Inc.

ICS BOOKS INC., MERRILLVILLE, IN

SKIING! Faceplants, Eggbeaters and Snowsnakes *A Guide to the Ski Bum Lifestyle*
Copyright © 1995 by Carol Poster
Illustrated by Calvin Grondahl
10 9 8 7 6 5 4 3 2 1

All rights reserved, including the right to reproduce this book or portions thereof in any form or by any means, electronic or mechanical, including photocopying, recording, unless authorization is obtained, in writing, from the publisher.
All inquiries should be addressed to ICS Books, Inc, 1370 E. 86th Place, Merrillville, IN 46410

Printed in the U.S.A.
All ICS titles are printed on 50% recycled paper from pre-consumer waste. All sheets are processed without using acid.

recycled paper

Published by:
ICS BOOKS, Inc
1370 E. 86th Place
Merrillville, IN 46410
800-541-7323

Library of Congress Cataloging-in-Publication Data

Poster, Carol
    Skiing : faceplants, eggbeaters, and snowsnakes : A guide to the ski bum lifestyle / by carol poster.
  p. cm
      ISBN 1-57034-030-7
    1. skis and skiing - - Humor. I. Title
    GV854 . 3 P67   1995   95-32767
    796 . 93 -- dc20   CIP

Table of Contents

Chapter 1:   Introduction 1

Chapter 2:   The Trash method of Ski Instruction 3

Chapter 3:   Ski Area Etiquette 11

Chapter 4:   A Field Guide to the Ski Slopes 15

Chapter 5:   Zen and the Art of the Perfect Wipeout . . .23

Chapter 6:   Knee Surgery: A How-To Guide for
             Beginners 27

Chapter 7:   Bubba Goes Skiing 42

Chapter 8:   You've Lived Too Long in a Ski Town If . . .48

Chapter 9:   A Middle-Aged Intermediate's
             Guide to Ski Racing 52

Chapter 10: Take Your Wildman Skiing 62

Chapter 11: Can You Pass for a Local? 65

Chapter 12: A Ski Bum's Dictionary 70

ACKNOWLEDGEMENTS

Some of the chapters in this book have previously appeared, in slightly different form, in the following magazines:

Network, November 1989: "Taking It to the Slopes," March 1990: "Understanding Your Teenage Shredhead"

Snow Country, July/August 1991: "You've Lived in a Ski Town Too Long If ..."

The Sports Guide, December 1987: "The Good Sense of Ski Lessons," March 1988: The Lighter Side Of Knee Surgery And Rehabilitation," February 1992: "A Dead-End Ski Town Questionaire."

I would like to thank Tom Todd and the staff at ICS for their patience and good humour, Steve Howe and the staff at the Sports Guide for having provided space and support for my writing, and many of my skiing friends including Chris Allen, Karil Frohboese, Laura Porakova, and Donna Todd for inspiration.

Chapter I: Introduction

The transition from normal human being to full-fledged ski bum requires a substantial amount of physical stamina and mental determination, but even former tax accountants and bank vicepresidents have succeeded at the task. Many researchers, on observing these lifestyle changes, have attempted to investigate what precipitates such odd behavioral adaptations. Several famous neurophysiologists have noted that a desire to become a full-time ski bum usually occurs after the brain is damaged by frequent face plants on hard snow during learn-to-ski clinics.

Becoming a ski bum is not easy. You need to trade your 1995 BMW for a 1978 Subaru wagon; move from a nice house in the suburbs to an unheated trailer hidden in the national forest near the resort; substitute GORP, pizza, and beer for California cuisine; and exchange your fashionable clothes for GORE-TEX®, polypro, and duct tape.

This book will guide you through the steps necessary to your evolution from occasional skier to full-time ski bum. The author is not legally liable for any Visa bills, lawsuits, divorce cases, car repossessions or bankruptcies resulting from your decision. Besides, there's no point trying to sue someone whose most valuable possessions are four pairs of rock skis and a rusting mountain bike chained to the top of the high-mileage 1985 Toyota in which she sleeps.

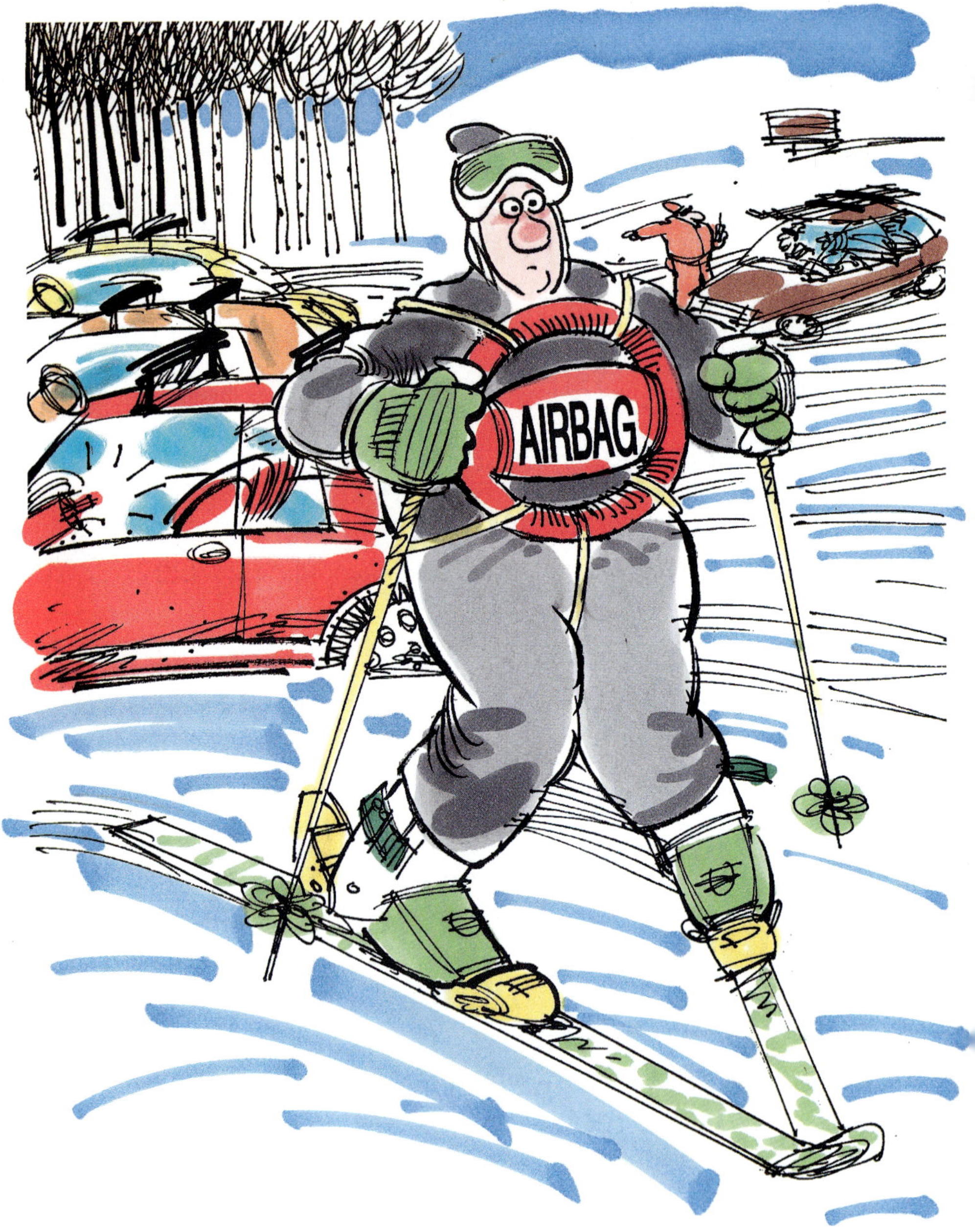
AIRBAG

Chapter 2: The Thrash Method of Ski Instruction

The first step in becoming a ski bum is learning how to ski. Unless you're a gorgeous blonde female, you won't fit into the ski community until you can cruise double blacks effortlessly while still hung over from a full night of partying. Although expert skiing is the cornerstone of the ultimately cool lifestyle, learning how to ski is distinctly uncool.

A basic rule of almost every sport is that all beginners are geeks. The only way to deal with this problem is to remain a beginner for as short a period of time as possible. You can improve your skiing two ways: on your own or by taking lessons. The basic choice is between an extended period of private flailing and a shorter period of public humiliation.

Learning the Hard Way

Twenty years ago, my friend Chris was an excellent example of why beginners should take ski lessons. Now, he is an example of why advanced skiers should take ski lessons. He skis like he drives. I think he's the only person ever to have gotten a speeding ticket going uphill in Parley's Canyon. (He's also a good example of why advanced drivers should take driving lessons -- but that's another story.)

Chris was taught to ski by a couple of friends when he was in the Navy. They taught him in the manner friends usually teach people. They showed him where to rent gear, took him up to the top of the lift, explained that it was easy, and left. Chris had no problem figuring out how to ski down the hill. He pointed his skis downhill, pushed off with his poles, and started moving. Changing direction was slightly more complicated.

Chris would ski straight downhill, and whenever he got going too fast, or needed to change direction, he'd choose a nice empty area and fall down. The snow was soft. He was enjoying himself. His technique worked.

He became over-confident. He had picked up a bit more speed than usual, and had planned to fall down near the base of the lift. Unfortunately, there was a long line. There wasn't enough room for him to stop. Yelling things like "WATCH OUT!" and "GET OUT OF MY WAY!" and "I CAN'T STOP," Chris sped through the crowd. Everyone cleared out of his way. He managed to get past the lift line without wiping out either himself or any innocent bystanders.

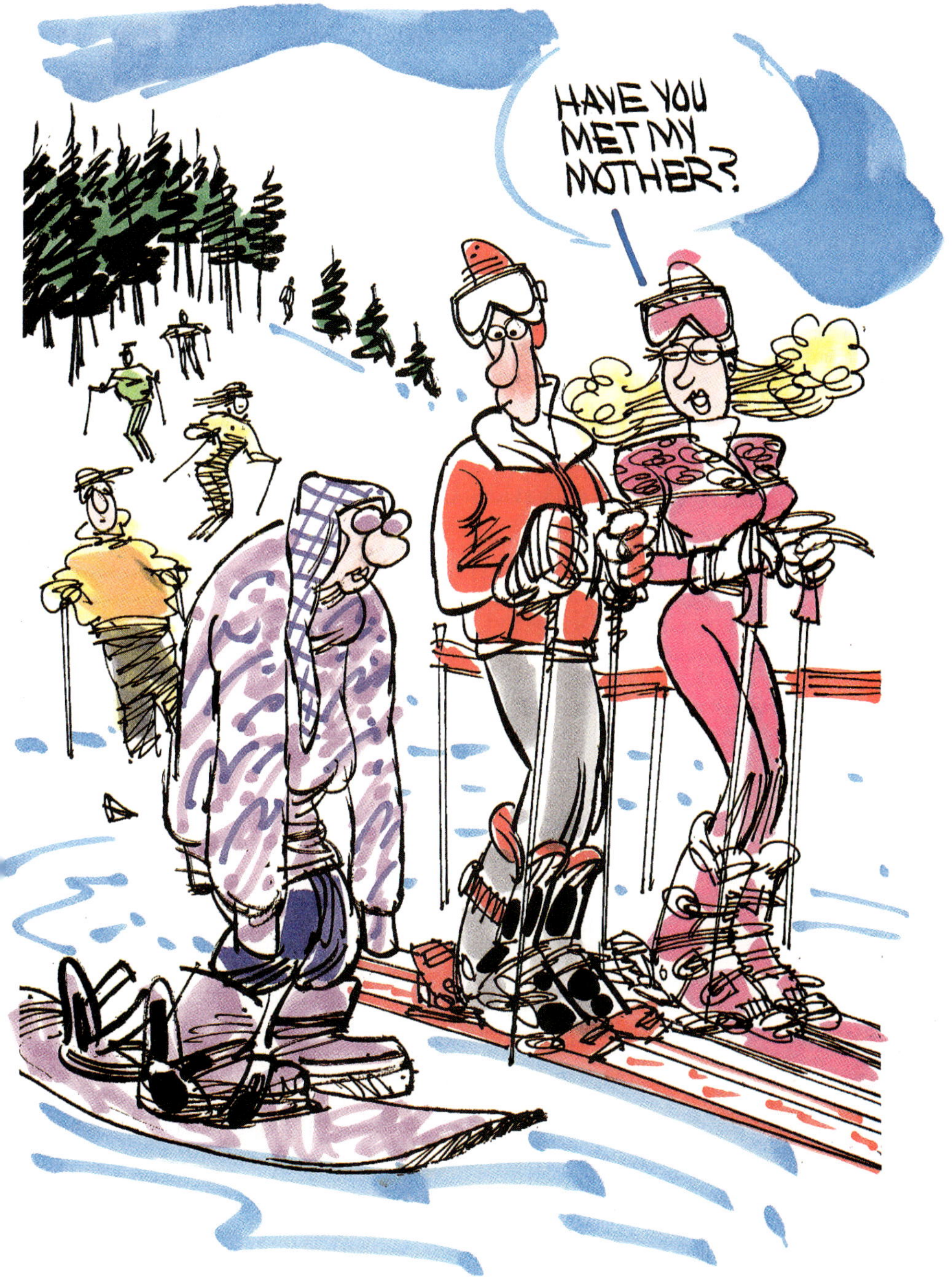
HAVE YOU MET MY MOTHER?

He saw an open area ahead of him. Just as he got ready to sit down, the slope steepened, and he started accelerating rapidly. By the time he got his breath back and he was prepared to fall, the slope steepened again. He picked up more speed. Suddenly, there was a small wood building ahead of him. He couldn't change direction. There wasn't room to slow down or stop. He was aimed at a closed door.

Luckily, the door was very old. When Chris' ski tips hit the door, it shattered. Chris continued on into the middle of the room. He came to a stop -- still standing -- in the middle of a room filled with a bunch of guys in uniforms. He had just skied into the ski instructors' shack.

Fortunately for Chris, the instructors were too astonished to be angry. Chris got his first ski lesson for free. The instructors showed him how to change direction and stop, mainly in order to reduce the menace to the other skiers.

Learning From Friends

If you don't want to try learning on your own, you'll need to find a teacher. The worst possible choice is your "significant other." I can still remember my second day of skiing. My companion of the time was sure he knew an easy beginner route down from the top of the Park City gondola -- negotiable with even the shakiest snowplow. Unfortunately, it had been several years since he'd skied Park City, and the easy route along which I trustingly followed him dead-ended at the top of the "ski team" runs -- pitches that appeared taller and steeper than Everest and covered with moguls the size of large

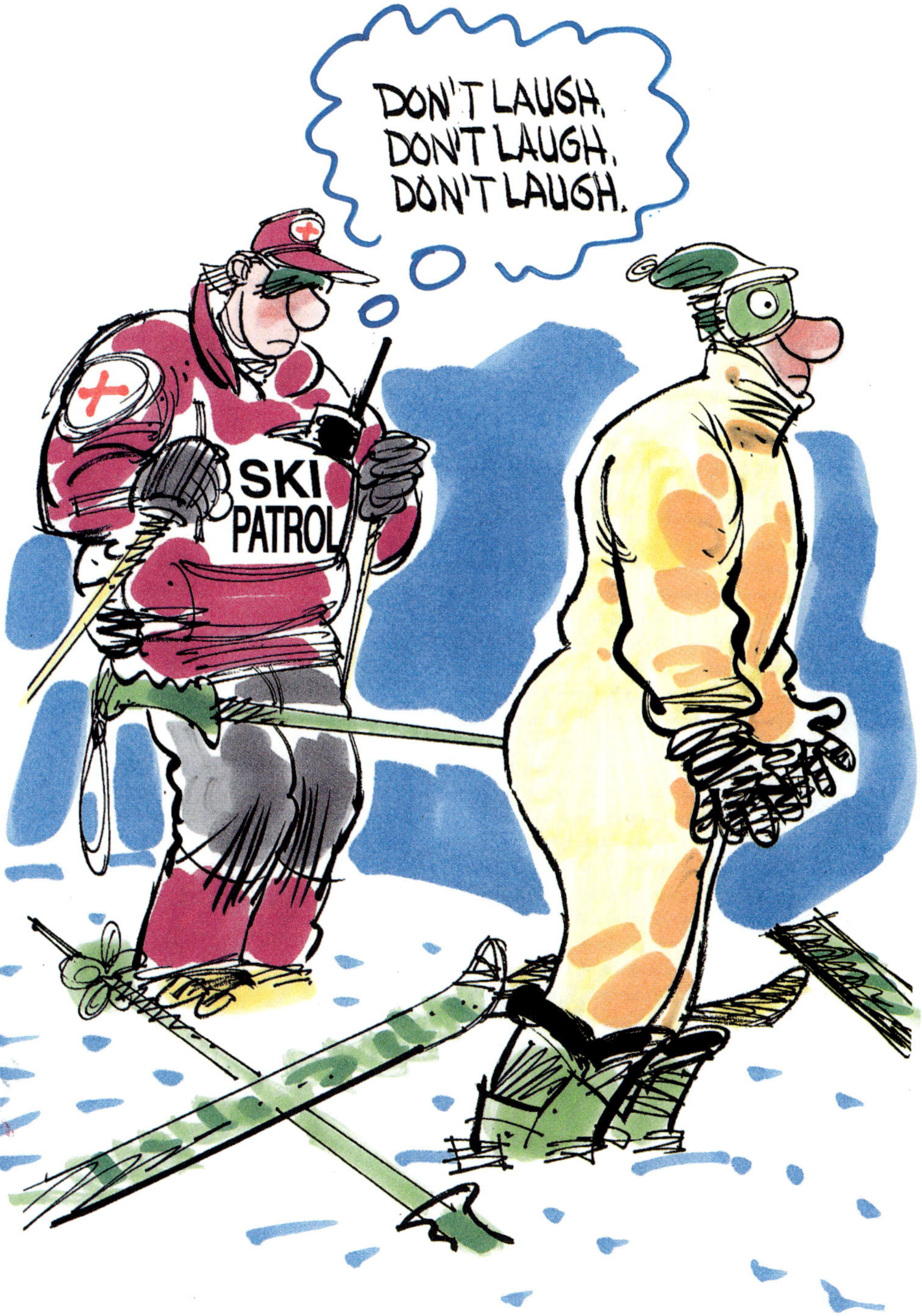
DON'T LAUGH.
DON'T LAUGH.
DON'T LAUGH.
SKI
PATROL

Volkswagens. By the time I'd reached the bottom, the only thing that dissuaded me from inserting my skis in a portion of his anatomy which would prevent him from sitting down for the rest of his life was sheer exhaustion.

Even the most well-intentioned friends can misjudge how pitches appear to a novice. I'd never thought of a golf course as containing killer steeps until a friend I was teaching panicked at the edge of a snow-covered sand trap, insisting that only a suicidal maniac would attempt the four- or five-foot slope leading down to the shallow depression in front of her skis.

Lack of teaching skills during your lessons isn't the worst problem with learning from friends -- it's lack of discretion afterwards. All beginners do absurd things -- wipe out entire lift line mazes, crash into kinderschool classes, or forget to unload from the chairlift -- but if you do one of these while learning from a friend, you'll never live it down. No matter how good a skier you become, your "friend" will always remember the time you forgot to re-buckle your boots after getting off the chair and came out of boots as well as skis on your first turn, or the time you sank into a tree hole and came to a stop hanging upside down from a branch by your skis.

Professional Ski Lessons

If you enjoy spending megabucks for the privilege of making an idiot of yourself in front of large groups of strangers, you'll find ski lessons almost as much fun as karaoke.

On the day of your lesson, you'll hit the snooze button on your alarm a few extra times, discover you put on your turtleneck inside out and be forced to strip and re-dress, burn your breakfast, lose your car keys, and leave fifteen minutes late -- just like a normal working day.

You'll try to make up time on the road in your usual manner, and find that driving at highway speeds on snow-covered twisting mountain roads is not a good idea. After digging your car out of a ditch, you'll finally make it to the ski area, just in time to rent equipment and run to your ski lesson.

You stuff your feet into the first pair of boots the rental shop hands you, grab your skis, and try to run the three miles between the main base area and the ski school meeting place. You discover that ski boots are not comfortable for running. (Later you will discover that ski boots are not comfortable for anything else either.)

Finally you are assigned a class consisting of an inhumanly good looking, deeply tanned, superbly coordinated ski instructor and a mixture of fellow students ranging from aggressive mountain bikers whose speed exists in inverse proportion to their skills to at least one terrified woman (forced into the proceedings by her husband) who panics whenever her skis move at all.

After you've mastered basic survival skills, you're ready to move into more advanced lessons. You're told to go to a "splitting" area where students will be assigned to classes based on their ability level. This is without doubt the most embarassing part of any ski lesson. A supervisor stands in the center of the hill and several instructors stand below him carrying signs labeled "A," "B," "C," etc. (This is school.) You ski downhill and are assigned to a class based on the worst ten turns of your entire skiing career. A special class is reserved for the student who bounces off the supervisor and then wipes out all the sign-carrying instructors like a row of dominos. Go for it.

No matter how uncoordinated you are in class, relax. Remember that ski instructors don't spend all of their free time talking about their students' dumb mistakes -- they sometimes talk about their supervisors' dumb policies. Also, once you've mastered advanced skiing skills, you'll never need to take a class again.

Chapter 3:
Ski Area Etiquette

An important part of learning how to ski is learning how to behave yourself on the ski slopes. A stunningly beautiful obviously incompetent young blonde woman may survive sliding out of control over the tails of two hundred skiers, taking out three lines of the maze, and stopping by crashing in the arms of the lift attendant, by smiling sweetly and hopping on the next chair, but the average skier attempting this maneuver will be pounded into the nearest snowbank by several dozen irate skiers and not recovered until spring thaw.

Ski etiquette, like driving manners, varies with region and resort -- and the only way to identify the idiosyncratic combination of freedoms and taboos associated with any given area is experience. For example, although western Canadians are as obsessively polite about lift lines as the British are about queuing in all its forms, they have no problems with fast skiing and massive air time, while New York teen-agers, who have been known to commit mass murder in order to advance a few place in a lift line, ski slightly slower than the average western grandmother.

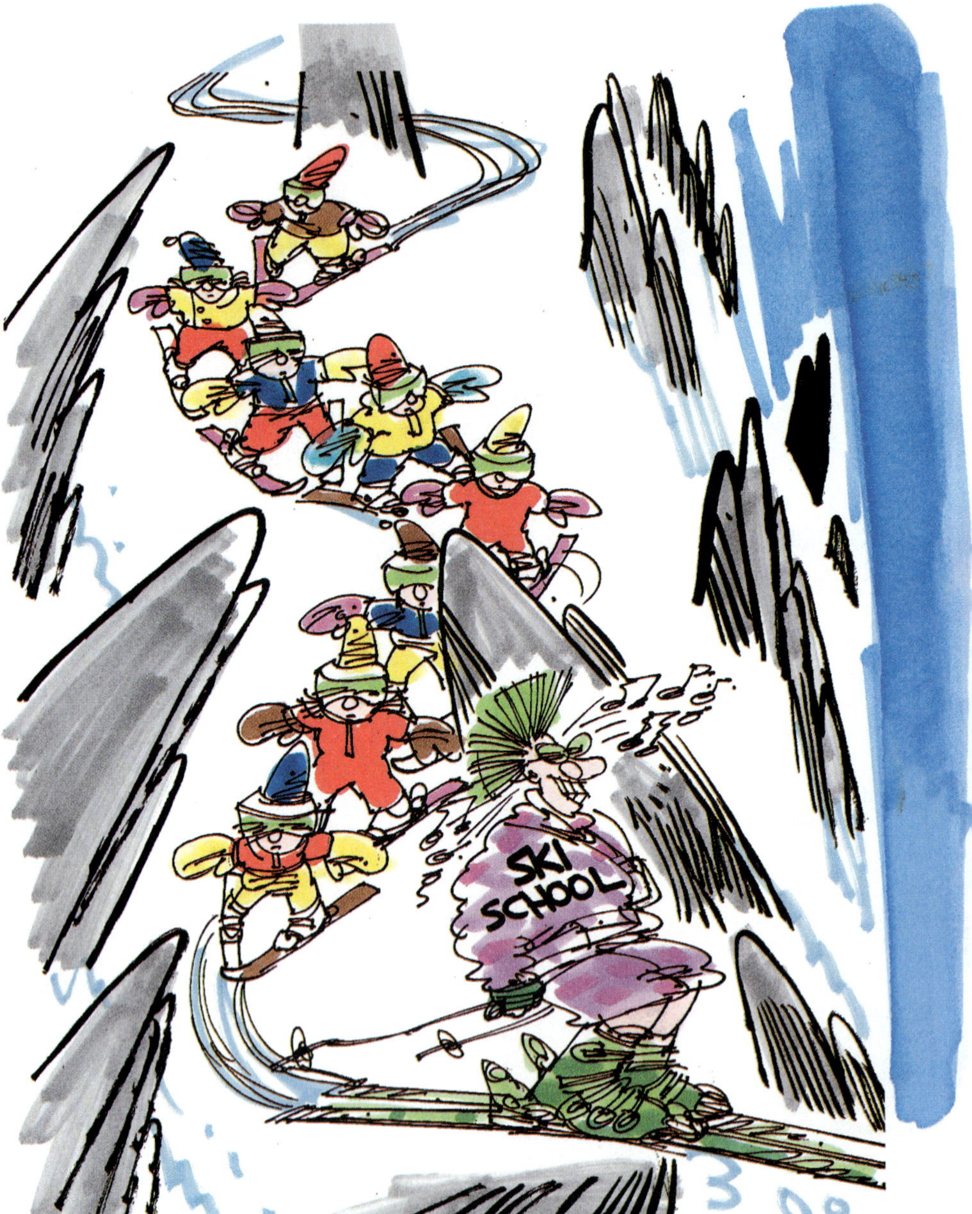

Despite regional variations, however, some actions are socially unacceptable at all North American resorts. Avoiding the following *faux pas* will go a long way towards making you an accepted member of the ski community.

DON'T:

Chew tobacco on the lift and spit at the skiers passing below you.

Use ski school classes as human gates.

Eat the cafeteria food (especially before a long gondola ride in a high wind).

Flip off lifties. (They're only doing their job.)

Plant poles on fallen skiers while bashing bumps.

Tell the patrol that they don't need to shoot a closed run because you've already skied it and it didn't slide.

Stick used chewing gum under the chair.

Collide deliberately with other skiers (unless they are members of a different gender and you are incredibly good-looking).

Jump "Slow Skiing" signs in sight of the patrol.

Ski over ground squirrels.

Yell wipeout ratings from the chair lift (unless they rate over 9.6).

Make loud gobbling noises at tourists.

Place obstacles below blind curves so you can videotape all the spectacular wipeouts that result.

Relieve yourself in sight of heavily traveled ski runs. (Go a few trees back.)

Race slope-grooming equipment on narrow runs.

Ask your chair lift companions if they've ever heard about the Mormons? And whether they'd like to know more?

Push Mormon missionaries off chair lifts (unless you're passing over a very deep ravine).

Chapter 4: A Field Guide to the Ski Slopes

Every ecosystem possesses its own unique flora and fauna. Ski bums should be able to readily identify the common species which flourish at most Alpine ski resorts:

Name:	**Bungee Jumper** (*Stolidus invertus mobilus*)
Tracks:	Rare high velocity contact with earth leaves roughly the same impression as Patriot missile.
Appearance:	Permanently bugged-out eyes.
Call:	Loud whoops terminated by sudden silences.
Where Found:	Dangling from hot air balloons
Feeding Habits:	Not advisable.
Scat:	Any food ingested in past 24 hours; eyeballs.

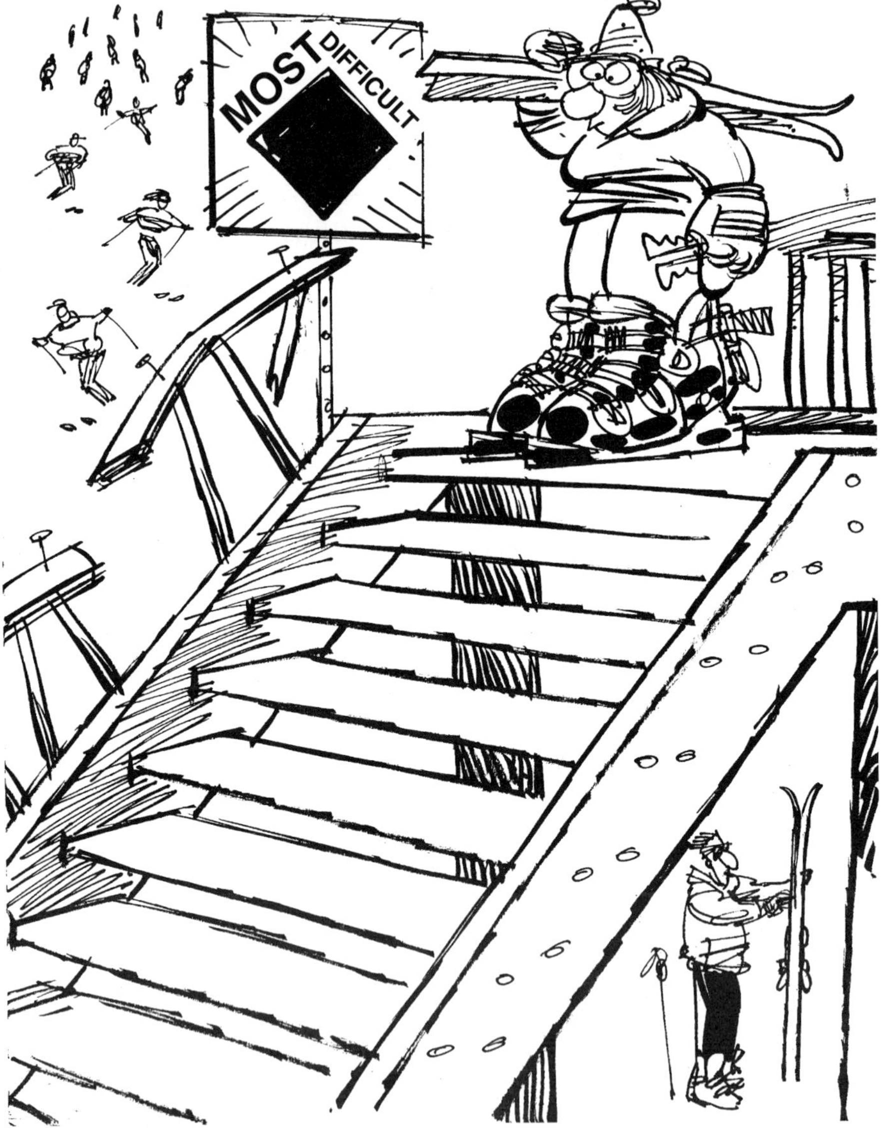
MOST DIFFICULT

Name:	**Extreme Skier** (*Pseudo-Plakus auto destructus*)
Tracks:	Figure elevens leading to nearest cornice.
Appearance:	Covered with brilliant and elaborately groomed plummage slightly disheveled by high-speed impacts into deep snow.
Call:	"Go for it, dude!"
Where Found:	Just outside area boundaries.
Feeding Habits:	Subsists on happy hour munchies at local bars.
Scat:	Broken skis, shattered goggles, bent poles, unneeded knee braces.

Name:	**Hardcore Snowboarder** (*Snowboardus vetus*)
Tracks:	Short tracks from board and occasional hand prints separated by long intervals in air.
Appearance:	Grunge.
Call:	"Babes!"
Where Found:	Half pipes.
Feeding Habits:	You don't want to know.
Scat:	Ugly chicks.

Name:	**Mid-Life Snowboarder** (*Snowboardus fa sus*)
Tracks:	Smooth (uninterrupted by air time).
Appearance:	Hair artfully arranged to cover receding hairline and subtly dyed to cover incipent grey. Turtleneck unzipped to show off full-body (tanning booth) tan.
Call:	"My last wife just didn't understand me."
Where Found:	Cruising the bars after the lifts close.
Feeding Habits:	Micro-brewery light beer and gourmet microwave dinners.
Scat:	Ex-wives.

Name:	**Mountain Bikers** (*Donor organus*)
Tracks:	Deep narrow ruts left by crampon equipped fat tires, punctuated by occasional craters.
Appearance:	Identifiable by huge thighs and shaved legs covered with scars.
Call:	"Jammin'!"
Where Found:	Steep, narrow trails.
Feeding Habits:	Eats dirt in summer and snow in winter while crashing.
Scat:	Tangled chains.

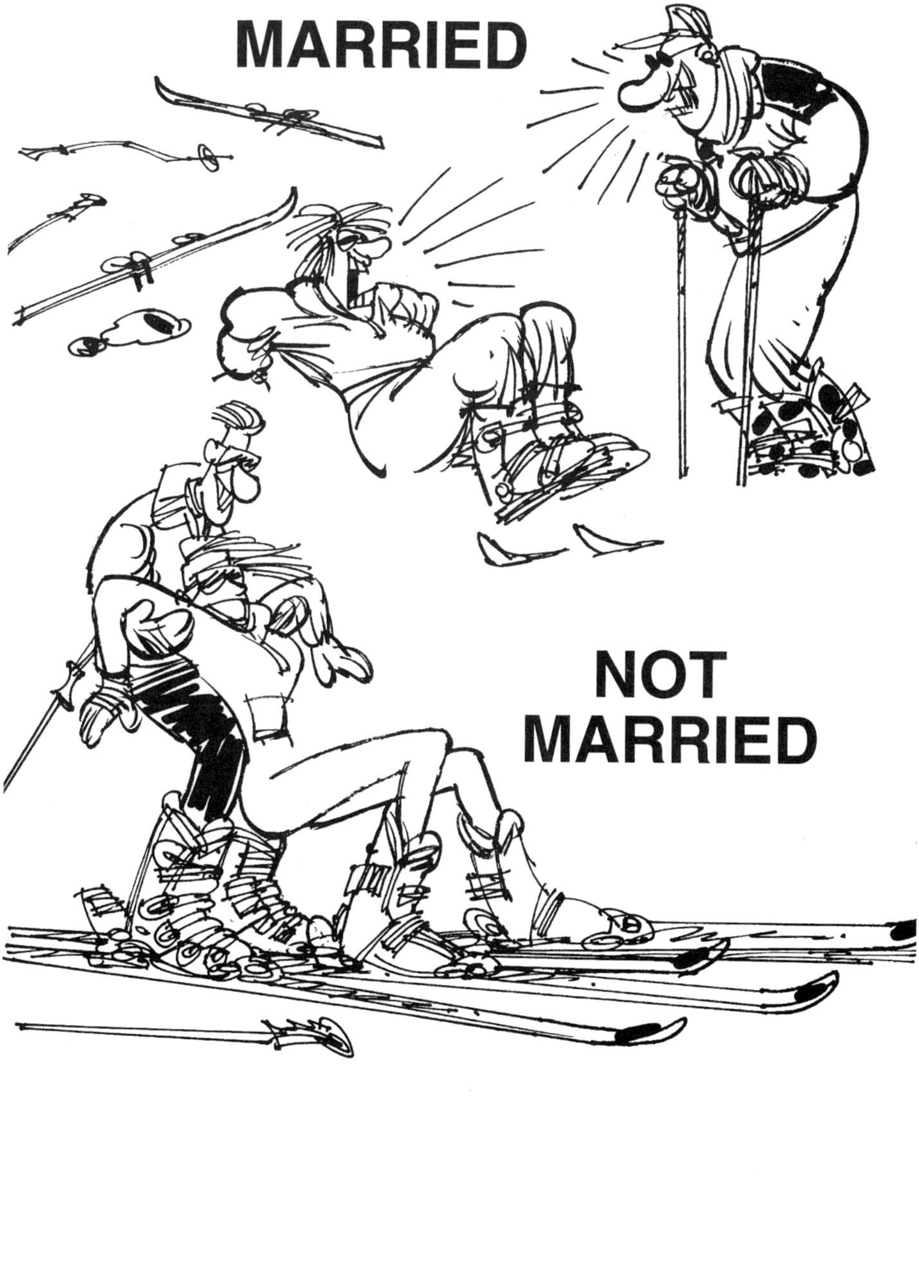
MARRIED
NOT
MARRIED

Name: **Parapente** (*Volacitus audax*)
Tracks: Large crater upon landing.
Appearance: A billowing cloth canopy attached to a trembling human by a mass of twisted lines.
Call: "Pink to descend?"
Where Found: Wrapped around lift cables.
Feeding Habits: Often catches birds in mid-air.
Scat: Anything not firmly attached.

Name: **Reluctant Wife** (*Femina timor*)
Tracks: Head directly back to the condo.
Appearance: Skis, boots, and new powder suit all color-coordinated.
Call: "Next year, we're snorkeling in the Caribbean."
Where Found: Shopping.
Feeding Habits: Prefers restaurants which serve the minimum amount of food for the maximum price.
Scat: Visa carbons.

Name: **Ski Patrol** (*Custodia montes*)
Tracks: Wide snowplow followed by narrow toboggan runners.
Appearance: Wears GORE-TEX® jacket with large white cross.
Call: Whistles loudly to attract attention of reckless skiers or attractive women.
Where Found: Getting first tracks on closed runs.
Feeding Habits: After having performed numerous recues of violently ill skiers, has learned to avoid the cafeteria food.
Scat: Pulled lift passes.

Name:	**Ski Photographer** (*Photographus natura implacabilis*)
Tracks:	Leaves distinctive tripod impressions beneath cliffs and on the side of race courses.
Appearance:	Invisible beneath backpack filled with camera gear, shovel for building jumps, tripod, notebooks, and press pass.
Call:	"Big smile!"
Where Found:	Just below cliff from which models are jumping. Sometimes misjudges trajectries and ends up directly below airborne models with disastrous results.
Feeding Habits:	Sneaks free food into camera bag at press receptions and lives on it for the next few weeks.
Scat:	Unsigned model releases.

Name:	**Skiing Celebrity** (*Notus flailus*)
Tracks:	Immediately eradicated by horde of followers.
Appearance:	Only form of slow skiing intermediate to attract thousands of specators without crashing.
Call:	"I owe it all to my parents."
Where Found:	Aspen.
Feeding Habits:	Probably quite ordinary -- but you'll need to shell out $11.99 for the cookbook to find out for sure.
Scat:	Autographs.

Name: **Slalom Racer** (*Cursor curcuitus*)
Tracks: Very deep ruts.
Appearance: Covered with more armor than a medieval knight and more padding than a hockey goalie.
Call: Rhythmic grunts as he blocks gates.
Where Found: Only skiers to deliberately seek out icy patches on steep groomed runs.
Feeding Habits: Occasionally swallows broken teeth.
Scat: Breakaway gates.

Name: **Triathlete** (*Askesis excessivus*)
Tracks: Deep postholes from jogging uphill rather than using lifts in order to improve the quality of his workout.
Appearance: Buffed.
Call: "Sure, I can handle it. I do triathlons."
Where Found: Fallen on steep technical runs where muscles don't help.
Feeding Habits: ERG and energy bars.
Scat: The bike on which he rode to the moutain and the goggles he uses for swiming laps in the hot tub.

Chapter 5:
Zen and the Art of the Perfect Wipeout

All skiers fall, but some put on a performance worthy of being immortalized by Warren Miller and others merely look hopelessly inept. The point system below will allow you to rate your own wipeouts and work on improving their quality.

Equipment lost:
- Goggles: 0.1 points
- Poles: 0.1 points each
- Parka or rain gear tied around your waist: 0.1 points
- Skis: 0.2 points each
- Hat or headband: 0.2 points
- Hip pack: 0.3 points
- Gloves: 0.3 points
- Neck gaiter: 0.3 points
- Watch: 0.5 points
- Sweater: 0.5 points
- Boots: 1.0 points each
- Lift pass: 1.0 points
- Knee brace: 1.0 points
- Ski pants: 2.0 points
- Turtleneck or long johns: 3.0 points
- Dentures: 4.0 points
- If completely naked when you finally stop: 10 points

Equipment spread: 0.1 points per 10 feet

Equipment damage:
- Lost bails (Nordic skis): 0.1 points each
- Bent poles: 0.2 points
- Shattered goggles: 0.3 points
- Torn ski pants: 0.4 points
- Broken bindings: 1.0 points each
- Broken skis: 2.0 points each

Damage to your own body: 1.0 points per $1,000 of surgery required

Air time:
- For every second of air time: 0.2 points
- For every 10 feet of air: 0.5 points
- Inverted (head down) air: 0.5 points

Length of nose furrow: 0.1 points per foot

Volume of snow displaced: 0.1 points per cubic meter

Speed at time of crash: For every 10 mph: 0.2 points

Time in motion after losing balance or gear: 0.2 points per second

Number and complexity of flailing manuveurs:
- Somersaults: 0.2 points each
- Eggbeaters: 0.2 points per second (add 0.5 points if you're wearing ankle straps or Nordic skis)
- Swan dive: 0.2 points
- Faceplant: 0.2 points
- Helicopter: 0.2 points

Difficulty of slope and snow conditions:
- Green circle: -1.0 points
- Groomed snow: -0.5 points
- Blue square: 0 points
- Black diamond: 0.2 points
- White ice: 0.3 points
- Double black diamond: 0.5 points
- Blue ice: 0.5 points
- Bottomless powder: 0.5 points
- Cliff area: 1.0 points
- Out of bounds: 1.0 points
- Requiring helicopter rescue: 5.0 points

Snow depth: 0.2 points per foot of loose snow

Collisions with natural or manmade hazards:
- Ground squirrels: 0.1 points
- Trees: 0.2 points
- Boulders: 0.2 points
- Lift towers: 0.3 points
- Stationary grooming equipment: 0.3 points
- Other skiers: 0.3 points each
- Cliffs: 0.4 points
- Streams or other unfrozen bodies of water: 0.5 points
- Moving grooming equipment: 0.5 points
- Elk or mule deer: 1.0 points
- Building roofs: 1.0 points
- Skunk: 2.0 points

Crater depth: 0.2 points per foot.

Visibility from chair: 1.0 points if easily visible

INTERPRETING YOUR SCORE:

Total number of points earned:

10 or over: Ready for Warren Miller
8.0-9.5:   Ready for home videos. Try for higher velocity.
5.0-7.5:   Good entertainment value -- but you need to try steeper terrain.
2.0-4.5:   Novice.
Under 2:   Get off the golf course onto the mountain.

Chapter 6:
Knee Surgery: A How-to Guide for Beginners

At first, you might have thought that people in ski towns did nothing but ski or talk about skiing all winter, but after a few seasons, you've noticed that the hard core seem to spend as much time involved in having knee surgery as in skiing. Chair lift conversations with veteran ski bums focus almost exclusively on orthopedists and physical therapists and are often conducted in an obscure dialect consisting of such terms as "ACL," "rehab," "terminal knee extensions," "manip," "range-of-motion," "scope," and "meniscus".

You begin to suspect that you will never be a real skier until you've blown out a few knee ligaments and accumulated several thousand dollars of high tech knee braces. Don't worry. If after a few seasons of skiing your knees prove indestructible, you can always try whitewater kayaking for a summer sport and total out a shoulder instead.

DOC, I DID IT SKING DOWN DEAD-MAN'S DROP.
NURSE, GO GET ME THE TRUTH SERUM.
ICE

Your First Knee Injury

Knee surgery has many of the same virtues as skiing. It is expensive; it requires large quantities of high tech gear; it's great exercise; and it satisfies all your masochistic longings. Most fun is the apres-surgery scene -- you take large quantities of mind-altering drugs legally.

You should plan on spending four to six months on your knee surgery and rehabilitation. During the first month, it is a full-time activity; later you spend two to three hours each day on rehabilitation.

Getting Started

If you want any real degree of sympathy from your friends, make sure to injure your knee while engaged in serious death sports. My friend Joel, an experienced mountaineer and rock climber, wrecked his knee stepping out of his car in the First Interstate Bank parking lot in Salt Lake City, and spent the next five months being asked, "How on earth did you manage to do that?"

Of course, the most dramatic way to blow out your knee is a high-speed ski accident, performed with all the panache of an Olympic downhill racer crashing spectacularly for the benefit of worldwide network TV. To insure Olympic-magnitude injuries in your own wipeout, set your bindings just like the racers do -- not to release under any conditions.

The Accident

If you're going to blow out a knee skiing, it's important to choose the right location. You have two choices: high-status runs or convenient runs. It's a choice between pride and practicality. The more difficult and inaccessible the run on which you wipe out, the higher the status of your injury. Some good locations are the Baldy Chutes and High Nowhere at Alta; the Upper Cirque, STH, or Mach Schnell at Snowbird; Rendezvous Bowl at Jackson; or The Plunge or Spiral Stairs at Telluride. Although injuries incurred when skiing expert terrain have high status, they do have some disadvantages.

First, you take off your skis and cross them above you on the snow. Then you sit and wonder whether you will get frost-bitten buns before your friends can fetch the ski patrol. The harder and less accessible the run, the longer it takes for the patrol to arrive and carry you to the base.

If you wipe out on an easy run, preferably under a chair lift, the patrol will show up in a few minutes and load you into a toboggan. Most ski patrol people are expert skiers, and they achieved their expertise as pro mogul racers. To maintain their high skill level, they need to practice constantly -- even while towing toboggans. Before you consider complaining about the quality and quantity of air time you experience consider the alternative -- snowmobiles.

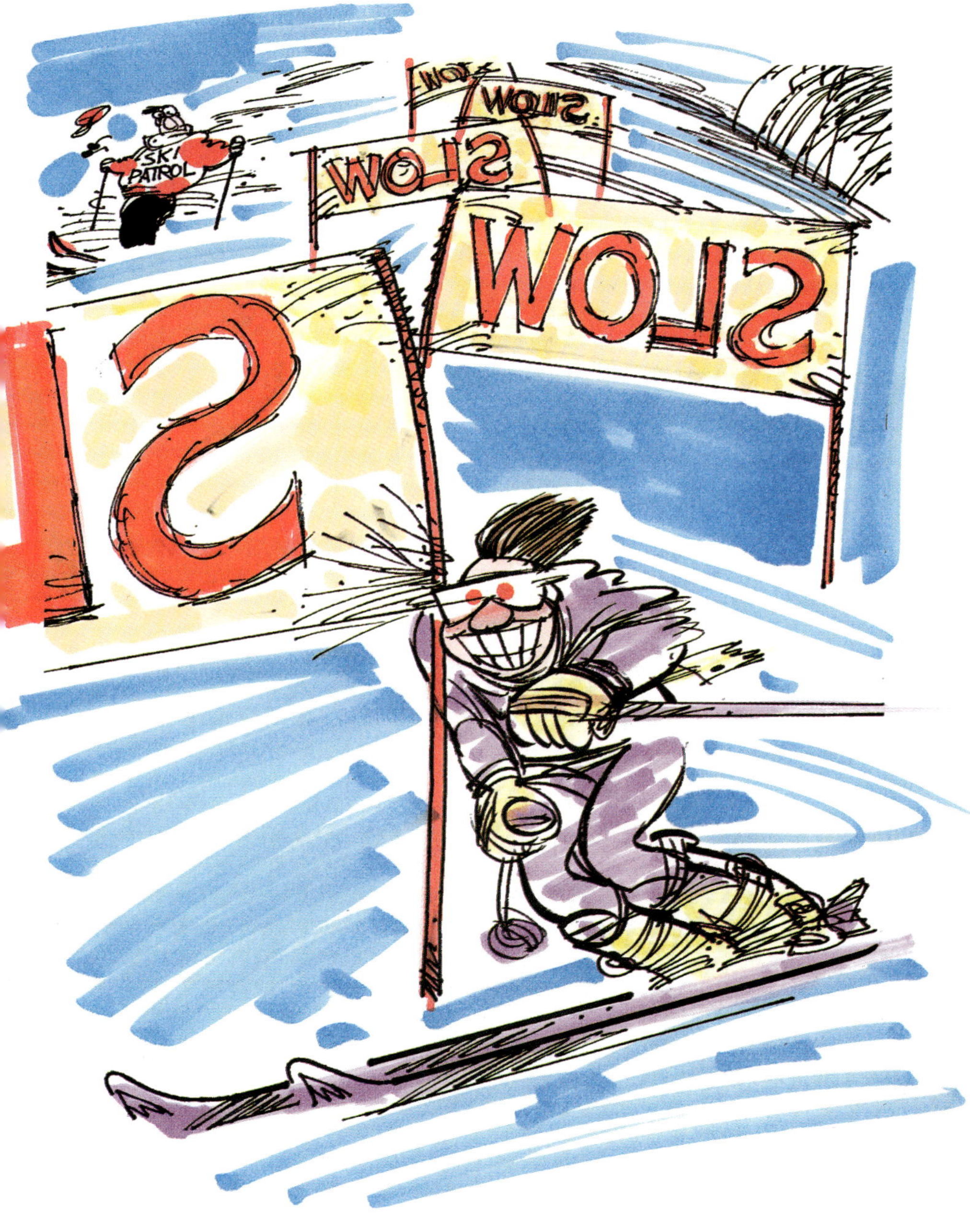
SKI PATROL
SLOW
SLOW
SLOW
SLOW

Preliminary Examination

The ski patrol carry you into a clinic or an emergency center. Someone asks you for complete details of your accident. If, as one of my friends did, you broke your leg on a bunny run -- you must admit to it. (Don't admit this to any of your friends -- you'll never live it down.) The doctor at the clinic will do a preliminary examination. If the injury is minor, you will be sent home with an elastic wrap and instructions. If the injury is severe, you will be given crutches, an elastic wrap or knee brace, pain medication, and a referral to an orthopedist.

As you lie in bed in the nearest clinic with a bag of snow or ice on your knee (this reduces swelling), you start working on the first of many logistical problems involved with knee injuries.

If you have been skiing with friends, you should arrange to go to a supermarket on your way home and buy a week's supply of food (unless you can raid the year's supply in your basement). Plan ahead. It may be days or months before you can drive again. If you have been skiing alone, you will need to find someone who can get a ride up to the resort and drive your car down. This is complicated. Make sure you have at least three friends with working cars.

Choosing Your Orthopedist

You have two species of orthopedists from which to chose: moderately rich and extremely rich. The moderately rich ones have paid off their first BMWs and are just working on their first hot tubs or swimming pools. The extremely rich ones own multiple BMWs and are working on multi-million dollar custom houses in the mountains. What you need to calculate is the implications of your orthopedist's economic status for your knee.

The less wealthy orthopedists tend to be young and aggressive, just beginning to work their way up in the profession, and keep abreast of all the latest innovations in order to create reputations as state-of-the-art knee surgeons. Before you let one of these guys work on you, realize that all new techniques are experiments. Then think about the newspaper reports on medical experiments, which always include such choice items as "fifty percent of the rats in the control group died."

The best orthopedists earn all their money from real estate investments, so they don't actually need to operate on you at all. Usually they don't. If you pay for a top orthopedist, you turn your knee over to a group of medical students under his nominal supervision. Nothing's wrong with these kids that three days of sleep, a gallon of hot coffee, and a sure-fire hangover remedy won't cure. At least you won't need to worry about being a guinea pig. The orthopedist insists his students use the same methods that he learned in school. What you will need to worry about is your surgical team approaching you in the operating room with a gallon of rum and a saw.

The Wait

If you're a new patient, it may take several weeks to get an appointment with a good orthopedist. While you are waiting, stretch out on the couch in front of the TV, use several pillows to elevate your knee above heart level, apply ice to your knee (fifteen minutes on, fifteen minutes off), knock back a few six-packs, put a ski film on your VCR, and feel sorry for yourself.

You have two choices about keeping in shape after knee injuries. You can start off with good intentions which will slowly evaporate or you can save yourself a considerable amount of trouble by stocking up on potato chips and microwave popcorn immediately. The only absolutely unavoidable form of post-knee injury conditioning is getting accustomed to crutches. You will need to build calluses on your palms and armpits on a gradual basis. (No one has natural armpit calluses!)

The People With the Thumbs

You finally get to see your orthopedist. Bring a book (an unabridged *Encyclopedia Brittanica* would be about the right length) to your appointment -- to be prepared for the wait. A nurse will escort you to a small room and settle you on an uncomfortable metal examination table. If you are wearing anything which covers your bad knee, you will need to remove it and change into a hospital gown the size and texture of a recycled paper napkin. A technician will x-ray your knee.

DID YOU KNOW YOUR EX.. HAS JOINED THE SKI PATROL?
IT COULDN'T GET WORSE.
SKI PATROL

After you have been in the examination room for fifteen minutes, someone will wander in and look at your knee, which will probably be the size, color, and texture of a large, over-ripe eggplant. That person will grab your ankle and thigh, and try to either pull your calf off or bend your knee sideways. (This tests ligaments.) After mumbling a few words in Latin, the person will jab a thumb in the sorest part of your knee and ask, "Does this hurt?"

Since you are writhing and screaming in agony, you may be tempted to reply sarcastically or even to kick with your good leg. Restrain yourself. Your orthopedist, despite a childhood spent pulling wings off flies and sewing them back on again in preparation for medical school, means well.

Usually two or three assorted junior doctors and therapists will jab their thumbs in your knee until your doctor arrives. Your doctor will proceed to pull and twist your leg, jab thumbs in your knee, and look at your x-rays. (To save money, bring any x-rays from the emergency clinic down to your orthopedist.) After the entire crowd confers for a few minutes, you will receive a diagnosis that makes perfect sense to anyone who has completed medical school.

Your Knee

Your knee consists of ligaments, bones, cartilage, and miscellaneous other stuff. You can injure all of these. If you have injured your knee very badly (completely ruptured ligaments, torn menisci), you will probably be subjected to one of two types of knee surgery:

Arthroscopy: The arthroscope is a small (one-eighth inch in diameter) periscope-like device that can be used to look anywhere inside your knee. Micro-instruments can be inserted in a channel through the arthroscope or in a separate hole in your knee. Generally, arthroscopic surgery is done on an outpatient basis, and the incisions are small enough to be covered with bandaids after a few days. This means that after five thousand dollars worth of surgery, you won't even have a scar to show for it.

Arthrotomy: If you want knees that look just like the knees of your favorite football star, this is the way to do it. The surgeon makes a large incision in your leg, opens up your knee joint, and inserts enough hardware in your knee to set off every airport metal detector in the country.

Luckily, you will sleep through your surgery. Unluckily, you will wake up afterwards.

When you wake up, you will discover that general anesthetics give a worse hangover than Ripple and Thunderbird combined. Be prepared for two (arthroscopy) or seven (arthrotomy) days of utter misery. You will consume more drugs than the average sixties college student, and everything will still hurt.

The Nautilus Nazis

Within a few days of surgery, you will start physical therapy. The difference between your surgeon and your physical therapist is that while your surgeon mauls you in your sleep, your physical therapist insists that you remain awake.

Two or three days after your surgery, when your knee still aches despite megadoses of strong narcotics, a therapist will march into your hospital room and start making you exercise your knee. You will perform two types of exercises:

Strengthening exercises: These are done with your fifteen-pound high tech knee brace locked in place and involve moving your hip and ankle joints in all directions to maintain your strength. They're tiring, but they don't hurt much.

Range of motion: Have you ever ripped the scab off a cut along with the Band-Aid? Imagine doing that a few hundred times, and you will be prepared for range-of-motion exercises. By the time you have finished six months of range-of-motion exercises, your knee will be restored to full mobility and your pain tolerance will have tripled.

Supervising all of this will be your physical therapist. Your physical therapist is a highly trained specialist who has spent many years studying his field and several summers doing internships in South American prisons. ("We have ways to make you do 5,000 more straight leg raises.") You must treat your physical therapist with great

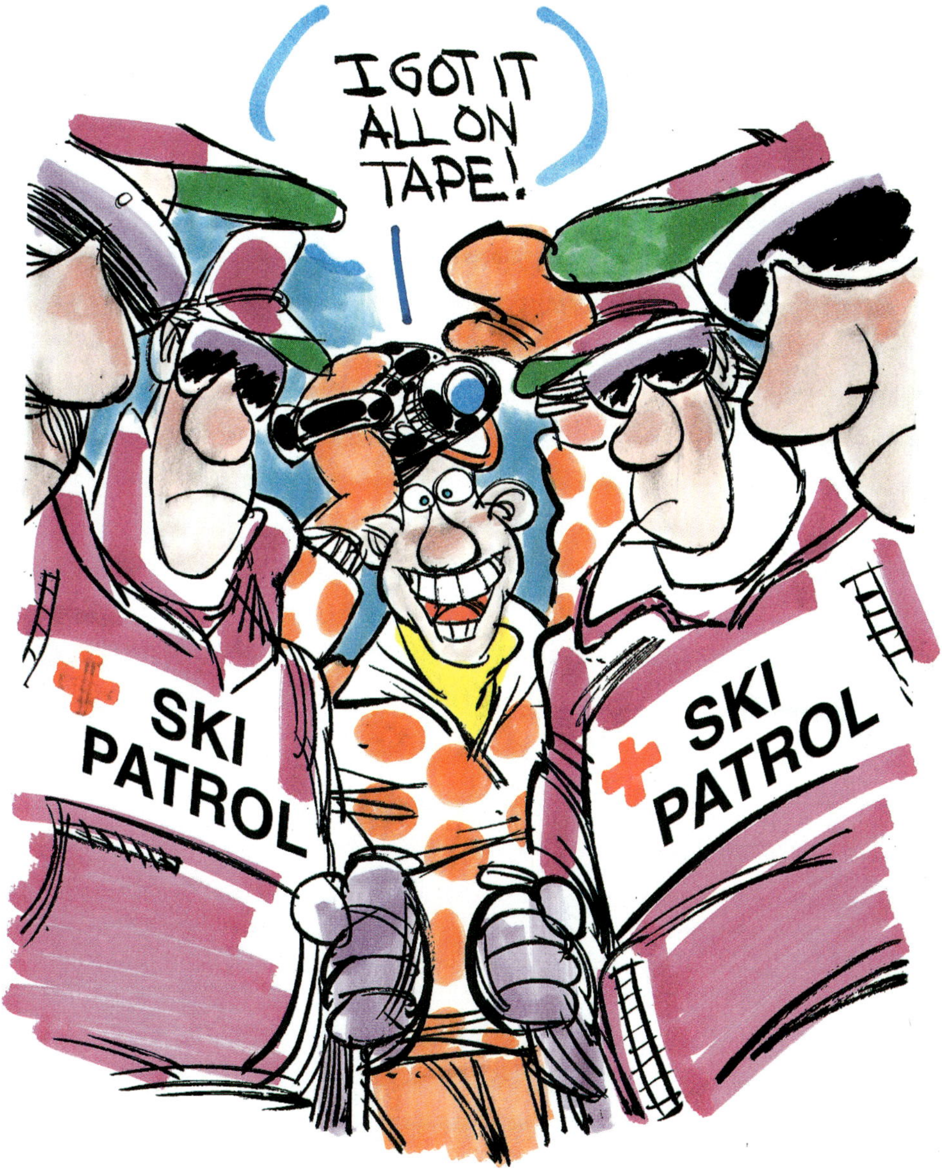
I GOT IT ALL ON TAPE!
SKI PATROL
SKI PATROL

respect at all times -- especially when he has his thumbs on your knees.

The Torture Chamber

You will be actively involved in rehabilitation for six months to one year after your surgery -- and you will be paying bills for six years to one century. The most important part of your program will be exercises you do at home two to four hours per day, every day. These exercises are designed to restore full functionality to your knee. If you don't force yourself to do them, your expensive ($2,000 to $10,000) surgical repair won't really help.

You will make weekly visits to your therapist. You will check in with a receptionist, then enter a room filled with machines ranging from the latest in computerized medical technology to designs which date back to the Spanish Inquisition. You will exercise on several of these machines, and both your strength and knee mobility will be measured. If you have not done your exercises at home, it will show. Not only will your recovery be slower, but you may be assigned more frequent visits to your therapist and the machines. Watch out.

Recovery

Every day you make some progress. You get more mobile on crutches, you stop needing pain pills (remember, it's not legal to pay for your surgery by selling left-over pain pills at rock concerts), you get another five degrees of mobility in your knee. One major milestone is when they remove your dressings.

Suddenly, your skin is exposed, yellow and dried from iodine, your knee swollen to twice its normal size, and the six inch gash in the side of your leg held together with large metal staples. Your doctor says "It looks good." You throw up.

One year later, your incision has become a scar, your knee is nearly as good as new, and you can return to the activities that injured your knee to begin with -- until your next injury.

Chapter 7:
Bubba Goes Skiing

Now that every fashionable resort boutique and suburban shopping mall are selling western wear, it gets hard to distinguish the real redneck from high-priced imitations. This quiz will measure your degree of authenticity:

(1) How do you combine nicotine and skiing?
- (a) Don't smoke.
- (b) Smoke cigarettes.
- (c) Chew Levi Garrett tobacco and spit from the chair.
- (d) Dip snuff and spit into an empty Dr. Pepper can you carry for that purpose.

(2) You deal with lift lines by:
- (a) Reading *War and Peace* while you wait patiently.
- (b) Handing out copies of *The Book of Mormon.*
- (c) Driving down the mountain throwing beer bottles at road signs to express your displeasure.
- (d) Having your old lady drive you up to the top of the mountain in your pick-up and meet you at the bottom until the lines disappear.

I KNOW WHAT YOU'RE THINKING IF HE CAN TEACH A CHIMP... HE CAN TEACH ME.
SKI SCHOOL

(3) For lunch you:
- (a) Go into town to try out the new Mid-Eastern vegetarian restaurant.
- (b) Grab a burger and fries at the mid-mountain cafeteria.
- (c) Don't waste time eating when there's still good snow.
- (d) Eat a Slim Jim and three Snickers bars that you'd left in your pockets at the end of deer season and plumb forgot until you put on the jacket to go skiing.

(4) Your favorite ski companion is:
- (a) Part of your business network.
- (b) Your spouse and kids.
- (c) You ski single because you like your powder untracked.
- (d) Your pit bull.

(5) You cope with dehydration by:
- (a) Sipping Evian from small plastic bottles.
- (b) Ignoring it.
- (c) Having a few Buds with lunch.
- (d) Drinking PBRs on the chairs, crushing the cans in one hand, and trying to toss them up on top of the lift towers.

(6) You consider ideal ski attire:
- (a) A one-piece Bogner powder suit.
- (b) Matching KMart bib pants and parka over a cotton turtleneck.
- (c) Polypro, fleece, and GORE-TEX®.
- (d) A red flannel shirt, bib overalls, a camo jacket, and a baseball cap reading "Everybody's pretty after 2 a.m."

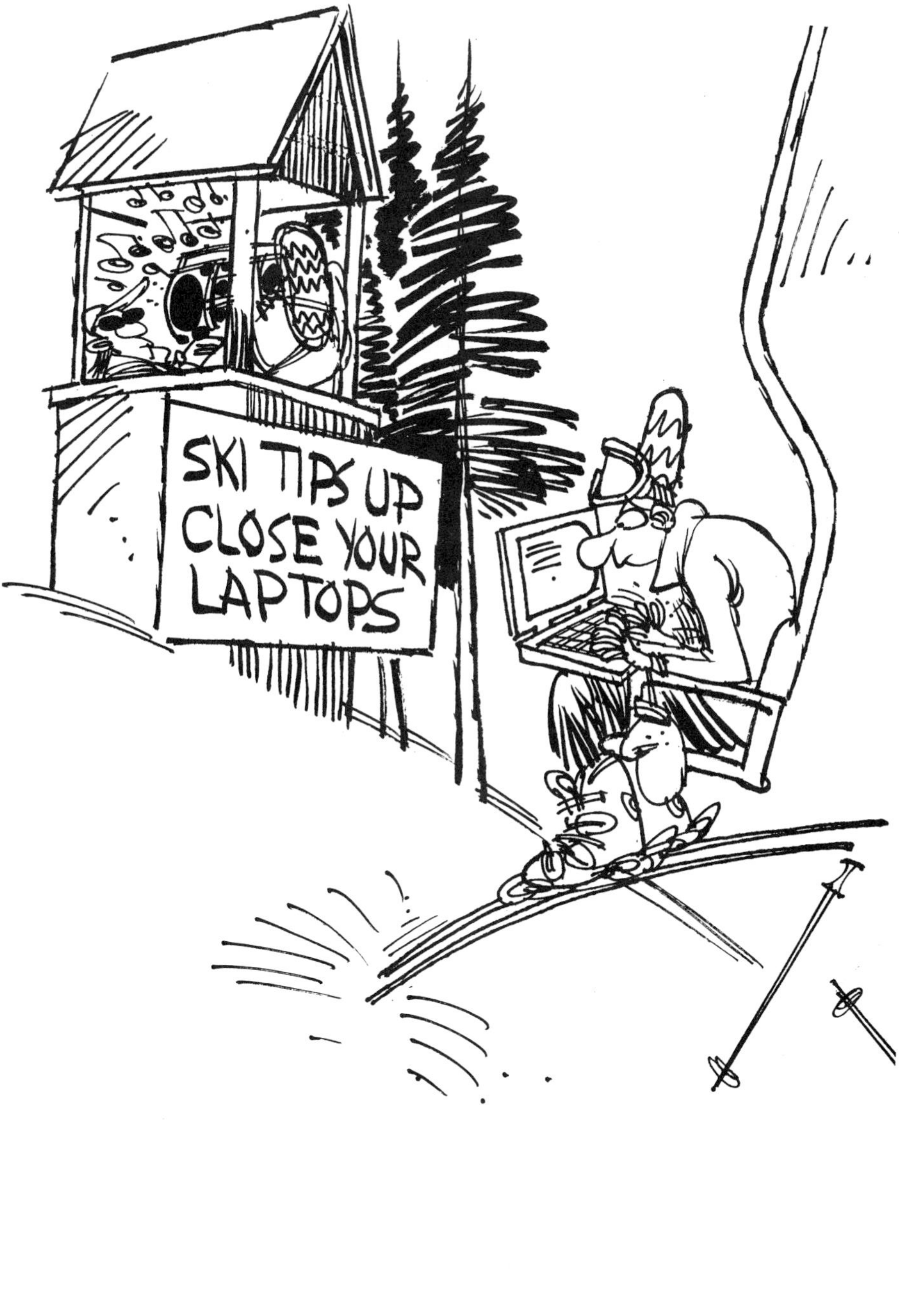
SKI TIPS UP
CLOSE YOUR
LAPTOPS

(7) When someone runs over your skis in the maze you:
   (a) Make a pointed remark to your skiing partner about modern manners.
   (b) Apologize for getting in their way.
   (c) Discretely scratch their tails with the tip of your pole.
   (d) Pound them into the nearest snowbank with a tire iron.

(8) When you see moguls you:
   (a) Carve them gracefully, just like you learned at the ski clinic.
   (b) Take off your skis and hike back up to the cat track you missed.
   (c) Finish your beer so it don't get all shook up when you go for massive air.
   (d) Figure if you get up enough speed you'll sail right over them, just like how you drive your rig when the road to your house gets washboarded real bad because the county refuses to blade it until you pay your taxes.

(9) You don't worry about getting pulled over by the patrol because:
   (a) You own the resort.
   (b) You never ski fast and you obey all the signs.
   (c) None of the patrol can keep up with you -- especially in the trees.
   (d) Since your Uncle Junior plea-bargained your last DWI down to six months suspended, you figure that for crashing into a "Slow Skiing" sign and leveling a few kids in a ski class before sliding to a stop, you'll probably get off with just a fine.

(10) After skiing you:
- (a) Go soak in the hot tub in your condo.
- (b) Wander around the town buying souvenirs.
- (c) Fill up on free happy hour munchies at the bars.
- (d) Plug a couple of rabbits with your .45, field dress them, and throw them into the back of your rig to take home for dinner.

SCORING: For every answer of (a) subtract five points. Add zero points for each answer of (b), five points for each (c), and ten points for each (d).

INTERPRETING YOUR SCORE:

Negative score: A yuppie buying western wear at Aspen boutiques is still a yuppie. Don't take your Range Rover off the paved roads.

0-35: The word most often used to describe you is clueless. You're a fairly average suburbanite, and your only familiarity with the redneck lifestyle is what you see on TV.

40-70: You're a typical ski bum, but with your ancient and unregistered car, poverty, and enthusiasm for rural living all you need to join the redneck community is to listen to more country music and buy a few chickens.

75-100: Just change your name to Bubba and burn it on your belt buckle -- if you haven't done so already.

Chapter 8: You've Lived Too Long in a Ski Town If ...

You know you've lived in a ski town too long if:

You've held the same job for at least two consecutive seasons.

All your skis are rock skis.

You can get a pro deal on absolutely anything -- including condoms.

You can spot Californians at 500 yards and avoid riding up with them while skiing single on a quad with 20-minute lines.

You can do multiple linked 360s down the freeway without either spilling the cup of coffee in your right hand or thinking about putting the coffee mug down in order to put a second hand on the steering wheel.

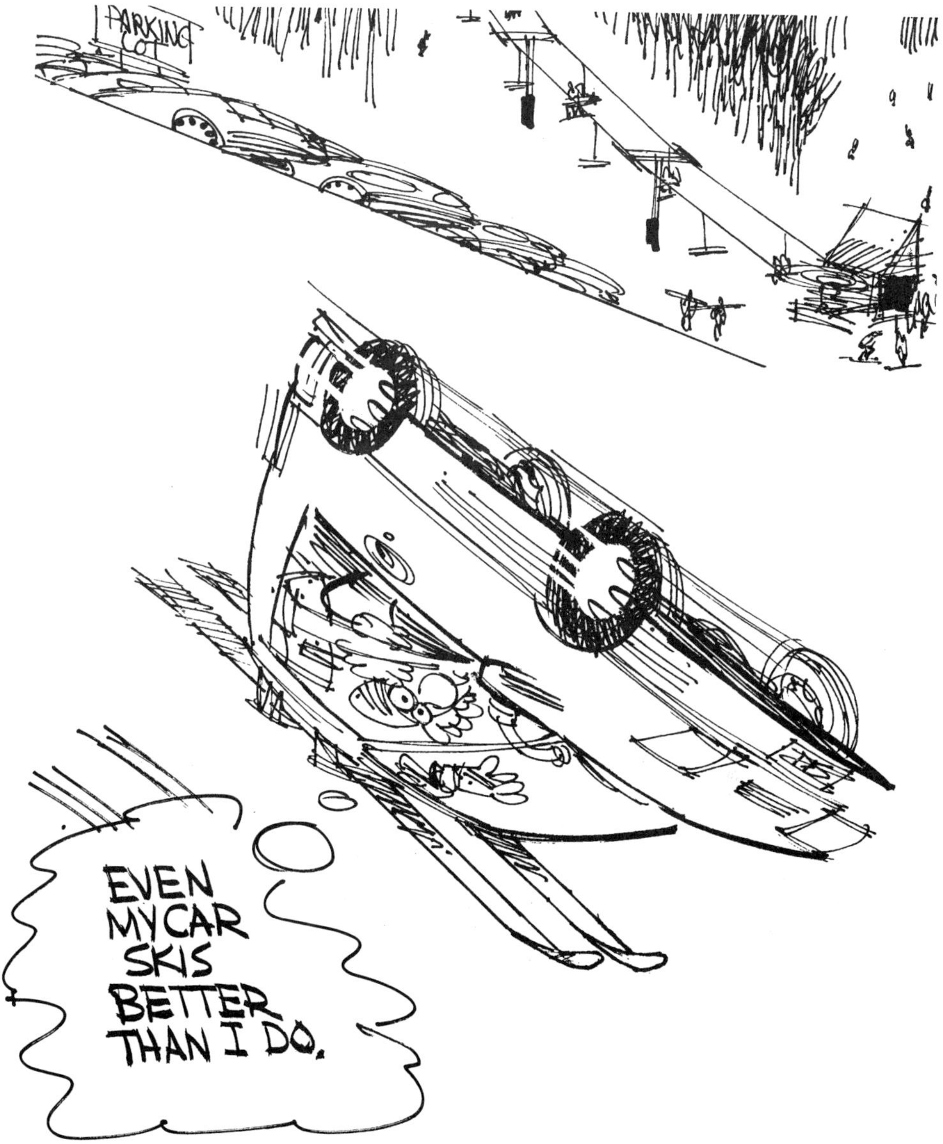
PARKING LOT
EVEN MY CAR SKIS BETTER THAN I DO.

You get kissed by lifties as you get on the chair.

You regard a purple capilene turtleneck, brilliantly colored Lycra tights, a pile pullover, and Sorel freestyle boots as ordinary street clothes.

It takes four weeks and several major crashes before you finally start to remember just where they cut the new road across your favorite run.

You unabashedly parallel on Nordic skis.

Sharing a chair with a movie star no longer surprises you.

Encountering a movie star who actually can ski does surprise you.

You routinely get first tracks at 10:30 a.m. -- without hiking.

You have marked every single rock at the resort with P-tex from your own bases.

You've accepted the fact that you never will try snowboarding.

Someone steals three pairs of skis from your garage and you can't tell that anything's missing.

You no longer find resort jobs glamorous.

You think that formal means changing into clean Lycra.

You believe that all houses come equipped with hot tubs.

Everything can be repaired with duct tape.

You haven't ironed anything since you dedicated your iron to hot waxing.

You refer to members of the U.S. Ski Team as "the kids."

You no longer need to work for your pass.

You don't know anyone who doesn't own a mountain bike.

You're not offended when someone calls you a pinhead.

You're bored with modeling for visiting ski photographers.

Your powder stash may be out of bounds, but otherwise it's completely legal.

You can equip up to fifteen houseguests with complete ski gear.

You single-handedly financed your orthopedist's last two BMWs.

You need to remove the gear from the Yak rack on your Toyota 4Runner before driving under low-clearance freeway overpasses.

Chapter 9: A Middle-Aged Intermediate's Guide to Ski Racing

Remember the last time you were skiing quietly down your favorite blue run, only to have three eight-year-olds run over the tails of your skis and then race off making loud gobbling noises? Unfortunately, you couldn't ski fast enough to catch them and beat them into a bloody pulp. You decided that you would never again be humiliated by anyone whose head was lower than your armpit, and you signed up for a week long summer race clinic.

You show up to the meeting area at 8:30 a.m., and find yourself surrounded by fifty sun-tanned athletic college students wearing what appears to be a cross between a plastic suit of armor and a hockey goalie's uniform.

You lean your 180s against a wall lined with hundreds of 223 centimeter downhill racing skis with names like "FACTORY TEST." One of the racers says, "Someone must have left their kid's skis here yesterday."

Five instructors, all of whom are the same age as your children, introduce themselves and escort you to the first tram of the day. Ominous signs inform you "THERE IS NO EASY WAY DOWN FROM THE TOP -- NOT RECOMMENDED FOR BEGINNERS" and "ICY CONDITIONS MAY EXIST. BEGINNERS AND INTERMEDIATES ARE ADVISED TO STAY OFF STEEPER SLOPES."

When you get off the tram, the senior coach adjusts his helmet and announces, "We're going to take an easy warmup run down Suicide Gully and see how you ski. Then we'll split you into groups based on your ability level."

Suicide Gully froze solid the previous night, and grooming crews have just transformed it into a minefield of baseball sized chunks of ice. It is obvious how the split will work. The kid next to you who skis like Franz Klammer will make it down with no problem and end up in the advanced group. His gorgeous blonde girlfriend who teaches aerobics for Jane Fonda will end up with the instructor who looks like a young Jean-Claude Killy. You will break every bone in your body and be taken down to the base on a tobaggon by the ski patrolman who looks like your Uncle Fred.

After The Split

You end up in the bottom group -- which consists of three ski instructors, a professional hockey player, two members of college ski teams, and the coach's girlfriend. All seven of them look in good enough shape to work as bathing suit models.

"Hello, my name is Bob, and we're going to ski together this week. I'd like you to tell me a bit about yourselves and what you want from this camp. Although we will be concentrating on GS and slalom, you'll get to run a Super G course later in the week."

After the introductions, Bob mumbles something about lateral projection into the turn and demonstrates by skiing halfway down the slope as smoothly as though the run was covered with packed powder instead of death cookies. You haven't a clue about what he was demonstrating, but you know that you have quite enough in the way of lateral projections -- especially around the hips. You make it down the hill without falling and feel extremely proud of yourself. Bob manages a sickly grin in your direction before explaining to Jean-Paul, the hockey player, that he might want to try turning occasionally.

Bob gets on the chairlift with the gorgeous blonde female ski instructor, and you pair up with his girlfriend, who mutters something about "dweebs" and spends the rest of the ride glaring at Bob. At the top of the lift, Bob asks, "Is everyone ready to run some gates now?" The college students are "ready to shred them" and "totally enthused." You ask Bob if you need to change into running shoes.

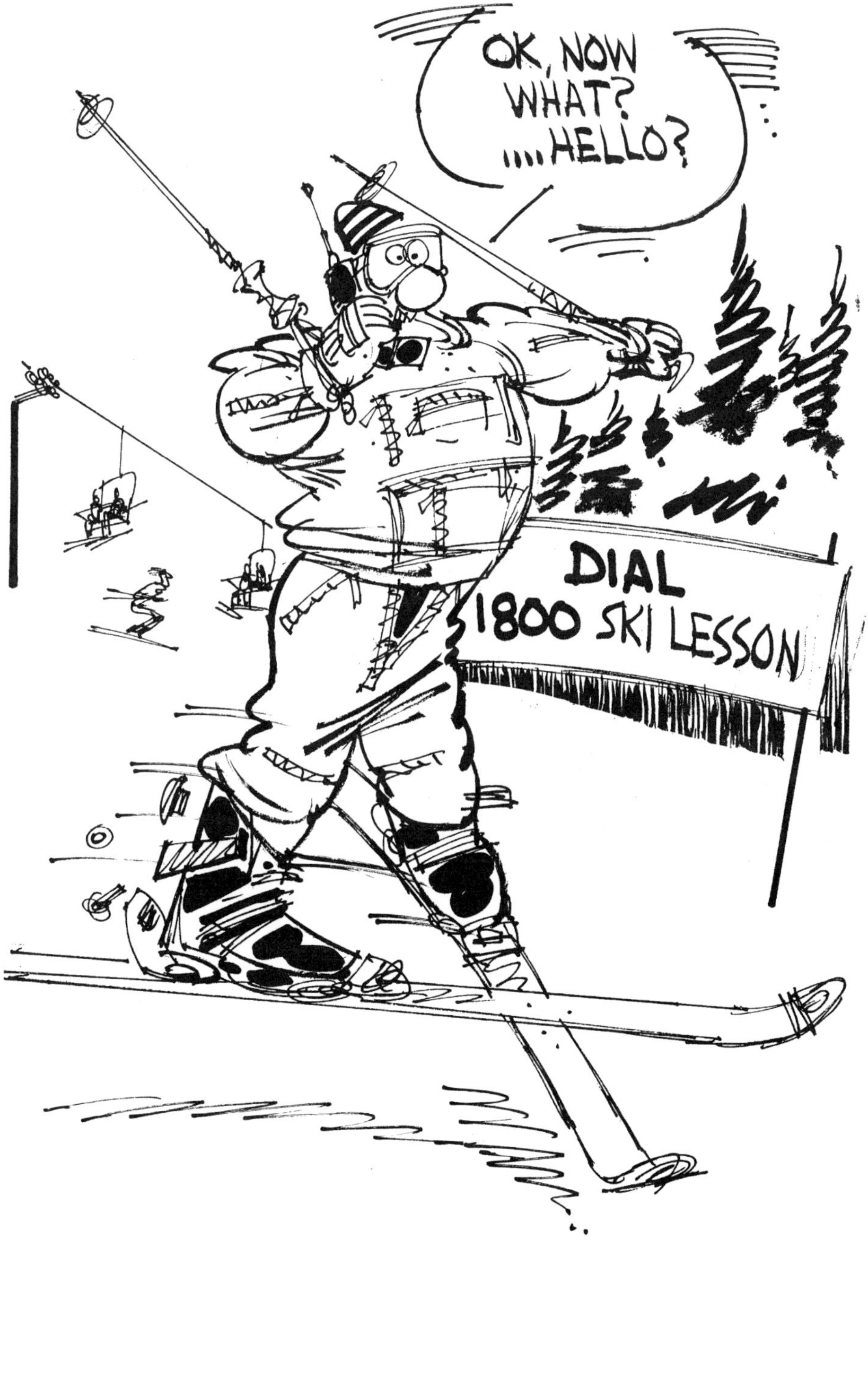
OK, NOW
WHAT?
....HELLO?
DIAL
1800 SKI LESSON

Running Gates

After ten minutes of technical explanations, you finally understand the theory behind "gates." The fastest way to get to the bottom of a slope is to point your skis downhill and let them rip. "Gates" are poles planted in the hill to force racers to make turns. They work on much the same principle as obstacle courses in basic training for the Green Berets -- and cause just as many injuries.

The college racers ski through the gates looking like Ingmar Stenmark on a good day. Jean-Paul firmly believes turning is for wimps. He points his 300-pound frame straight down the hill in a deep tuck and flattens one entire practice course. You discover that a cautious snowplow slows you down enough so you can actually turn around the few bamboo poles left intact by the previous skier without hitting anything.

The course looks less intimidating on your second run. You pole hard, pick up some speed, turn around the first gate, and look ahead. There is a gully, slightly wider and deeper than the Grand Canyon, in the spot where 200 aspiring racers have been turning. This must be one of the "ruts" about which the instructor warned his girlfriend. Gravity inexorably pulls you downhill. You notice chatter marks the size of your porch steps. You don't want to submit your aging and arthritic knees to this phenomenon, but neither do you want to embarrass yourself by skiing out of the course.

At the last moment you notice a thin strip of smooth snow between the rut and the gate. You steer your outside ski just to the inside of the rut and roll your ski onto its edge, with all the *elan* of a genuine racer. While your outside ski carves an elegant arc around the gate, the tip of your inside ski grabs the other side of the gate. Your bindings release, your poles fly from your hands, and you and the gate slide out of the course in an undignified heap. You have just mastered one of the essential racing moves -- "hooking a gate."

Skating, the next racing move you learn, has a great deal in common with snowplowing. The first obvious similarity is when your instructor skates he looks as graceful as Baryshnikov dancing the *Corsair*, and when students skate they look like spastic gorillas. Remember when you learned to snowplow and spent the next three months crossing your tips? When you learn skating, you spend hours crossing your tails. *Plus sa change, plus c'est la meme chose.*

Special Treats

The next day, Bob offers your class the opportunity to run a Super G course. The other students, all clad in more body armor than medieval knights, yell enthusiastically. You manage a sickly grin.

The Super G course is set on what looks like a five-mile-long sheet of glare ice tilted at an eighty-nine-degree angle. The ice is so clear that you can see frozen ground squirrels ten inches below the surface. The gates are set at intervals several hundred yards apart. Bob announces, cheerfully, "All you need to do is point your skis downhill and let them run." The other students take off at Mach 10, whooping enthusiastically.

You stand at the start whimpering pathetically. You realize that you either must ski down or hike back up to the tram. Your knees start trembling so much that your edges lose contact with the snow. You're sliding downhill into the course. You keep on trying to grab the gates to slow down, but you're moving too fast. The hill flattens. Your knees hit your chin, and it's over. You've run your first Super G and survived the experience.

Final Day

Everyone in the clinic is divided into teams for the final race. It reminds you how little has changed since elementary school -- you still get selected last.

Pride overcomes common sense, and you skate aggressively to the first gate of the dual slalom course. You turn, skate to the next gate still even with your opponent, and actually ride the rut, skis chattering like an ancient pickup on a washboarded Jeep trail. For the next gate, you aim slightly to the inside of the rut. You pick up speed -- slightly ahead of your opponent.

You're in the highly angulated stance you've just learned, and your skis are widely separated. You reach the gate. Your inside tip hooks the gate. The ski flies off into the air. The bamboo gate cracks. You sail into your opponent's course. He reaches his next gate at precisely the same time that you do. You, your opponent, and the gate slide out of the course intertwined like two fornicating octopi. Your remaining ski, both his skis, four poles, goggles, and miscellaneous pieces of equipment disengage themselves from your bodies and scatter across the snow.

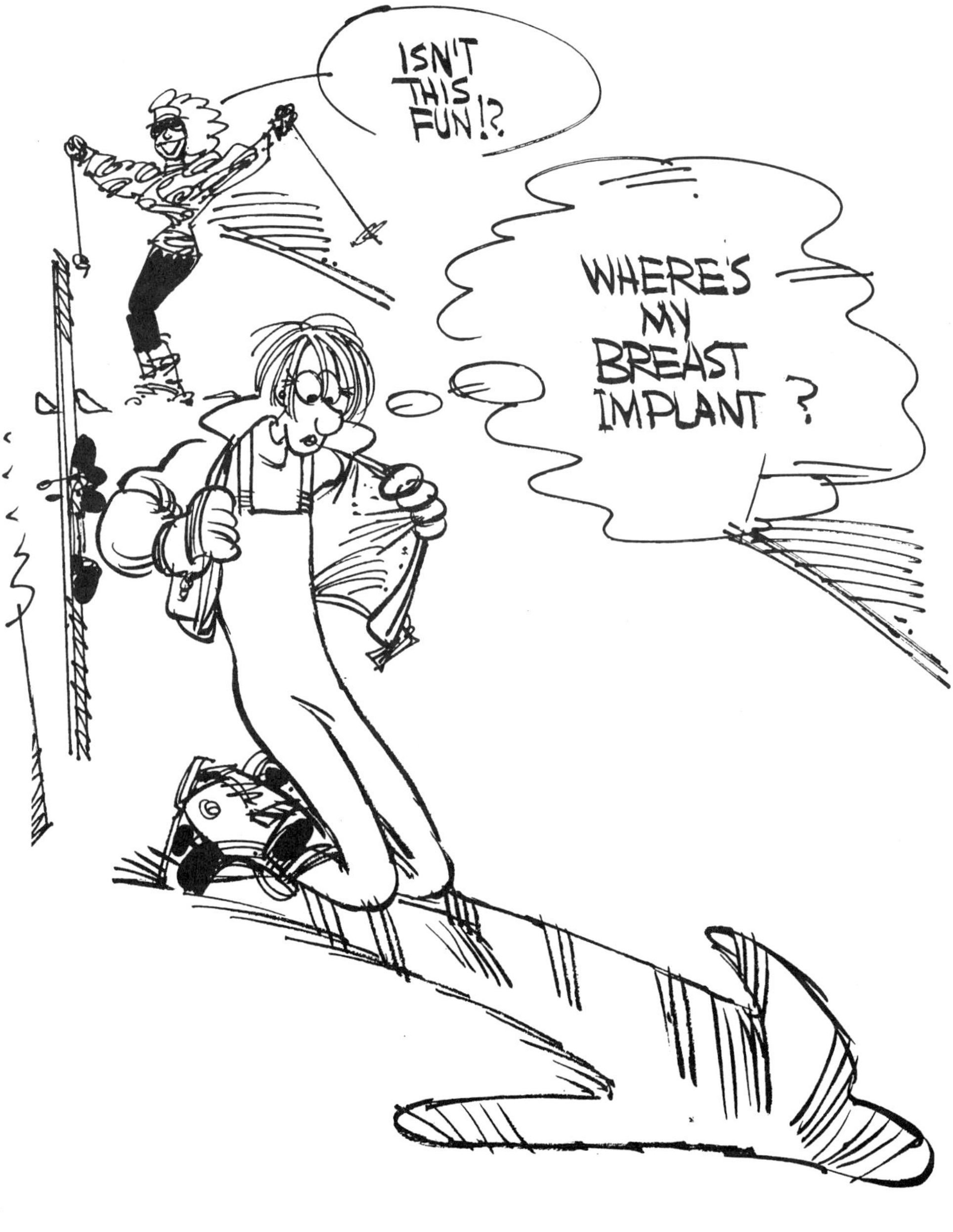
ISN'T THIS FUN!?
WHERE'S MY BREAST IMPLANT ?

You're out of control, sliding across the snow, intimately entangled with a man whose name you don't know. You look up and see a tripod. Then you skid over the tripod and finally come to a stop, wedged hard against the race photographer. The entire crowd bursts into enthusiastic applause.

You retrieve your gear and ski confidently down to the lift. After a week long clinic, you may not have become the world's best racer, but you've certainly managed a world-class wipeout, and you know that after this experience no mere punk kids will ever be able to intimidate you on the ski slopes again.

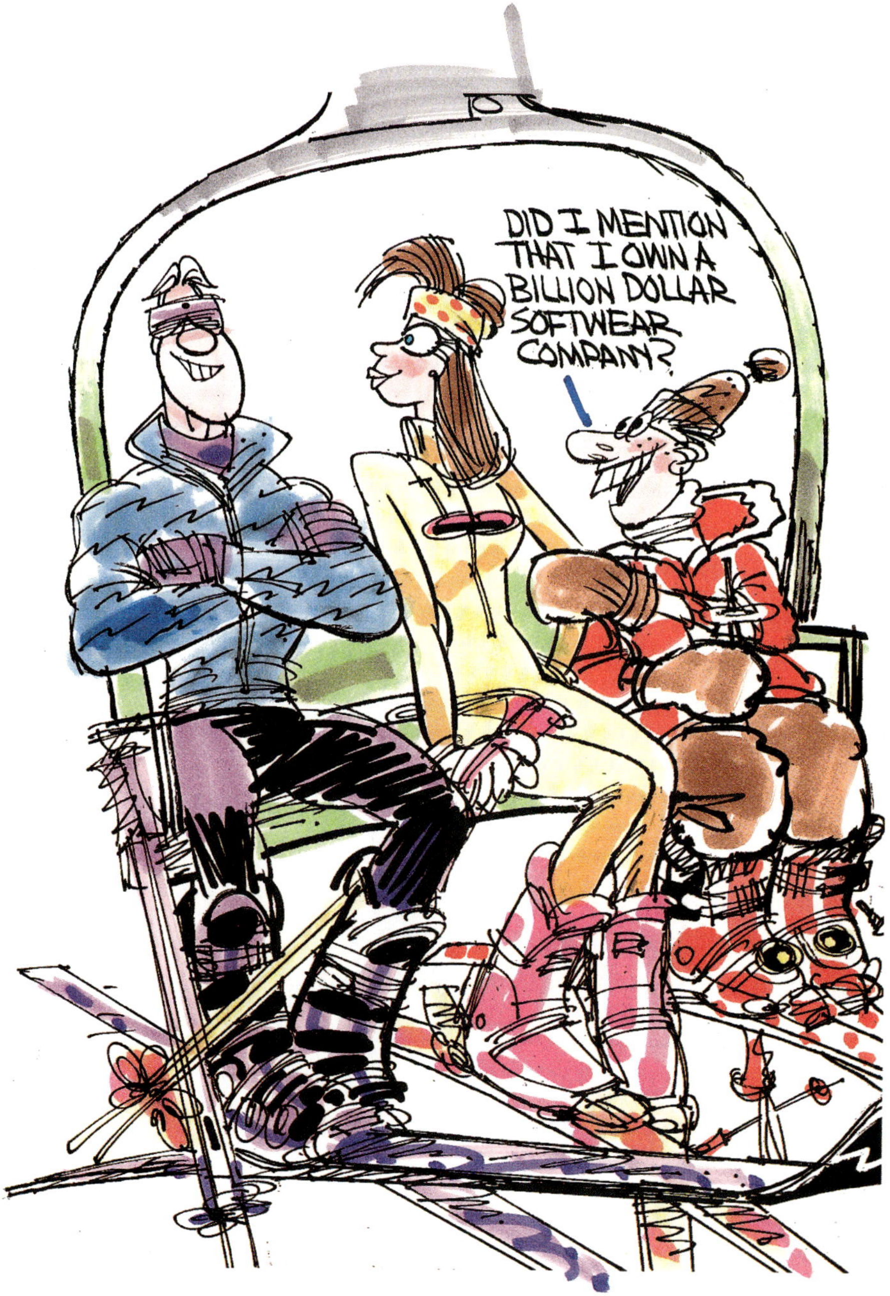
DID I MENTION THAT I OWN A BILLION DOLLAR SOFTWEAR COMPANY?

Chapter 10: Take Your Wildman Skiing:

10 Tips for Getting in Touch With Your Own Masculinity While Going for Big Air in the Bumps

(1) Dip snuff and spit from the chair to express your warrior nature. (It's okay to nail snowboarders, but aiming at elderly ladies, small children, or the handicapped is unsporting.)

(2) Discover a positive energy vortex when you pull off into the trees to urinate. Draw a big yellow peace sign on it.

(3) When you see a fallen skier, go up and share your experiences about falling with him. He'll feel better.

(4) Wear pink lycra and 223-centimeter downhill skis.

(5) It's acceptable to collide with other skiers at high speeds, but don't intrude on their personal space.

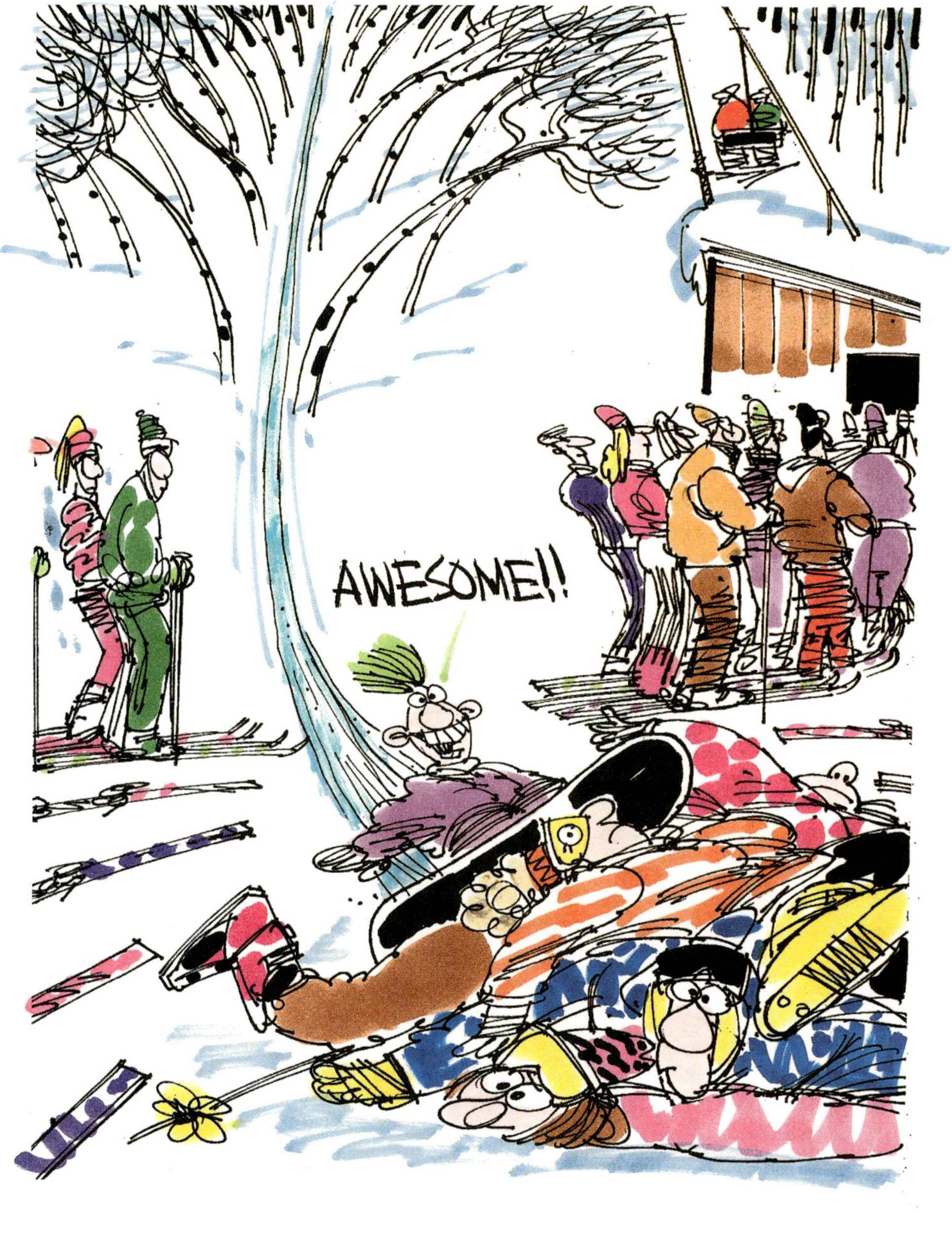
AWESOME!!

(6) If you're riding a gondola with other males, take your clothes off as a male bonding activity. If you're riding a gondola with an attractive single female skier, try this only if you have a very good body.

(7) When you wipe out, cry. It will express your wounded inner child. (Since you will be indistinguishable from numerous other skiers expressing their wounded outer children, no one will stop and ask embarrassing questions.)

(8) Eat the cafeteria hamburger raw to get in touch with your primitive nature (and save your arteries from the grease). Then belch (without apologizing).

(9) If you're riding on a chair lift with another man, express your feelings by hugging him. (If you're skiing a western resort, make sure he's not a local rancher before attempting this.)

(10) Carry drums.

Chapter 11: Can You Pass for a Local?

Skiing skills are an essential part of the ski scene, but to become a genuine ski bum you also need a considerable amount of arcane knowledge of ski culture and manners. This quiz tests your knowledge of the ski scene.

(1) A pieps is:
    (a) An instrument used in New Age music.
    (b) A small rodent that lives on scree slopes and emits high-pitched musical chirps when frightened.
    (c) A small radio transmitter carried by responsible back country skiers.

(2) Moguls are formed by:
    (a) Volkswagens buried on the slope at the beginning of the season.
    (b) Collapsed snowsnake tunnels.
    (c) Thousands of skiers crashing in precisely the same spot.

(3) Death cookies are:
   (a) Served with Kool-Aid by weird religious cults.
   (b) Called oatmeal-raisin at the mid-mountain cafeteria.
   (c) Created for your skiing pleasure by the resort's shiny new snowcat.

(4) Snow grooming involves:
   (a) Eyeshadow, lipstick, hairspray, and a $1,000 powder suit.
   (b) An array of expensive state-of-the art machinery precisely deployed to transform the worst possible snow into an ideal skiing surface.
   (c) Flattening out all available powder so intermedates can ski slopes too steep for them.

(5) A powder hound is:
   (a) A specially trained dog used by U.S. Customs agents to detect smuggled drugs.
   (b) A specially trained dog used by the ski patrol to locate missing skiers.
   (c) A skier specially trained to locate untracked powder at 3:00 p.m. at a crowded resort.

(6) Packed powder refers to:
   (a) A granola bar carried in a skier's fanny pack through several hundred spectacular crashes.
   (b) Fresh snow groomed to the texture of velvet.
   (c) No new snow for the past eight weeks.

(7) A ski-in ski-out condo refers to:
- (a) A condo close to the ski area base.
- (b) Lodging constantly invaded by out-of-control skiers hurtling through windows and crashing into the hot tub.
- (c) The only method you'll be able to use to get from your condo to anyplace in town until the snow under which the plows buried your car melts.

(8) You can legitimately complain about ice when:
- (a) There's too much in your soft drink.
- (b) You actually need to use your edges at a western resort.
- (c) You can see the frozen ground squirrels two feet below the surface of the slope.

(9) A snowplow is:
- (a) Used to clear the road up to the resort.
- (b) A manuveur used to control speed by beginning skiers.
- (c) Usually too big to jump, but if it's heading up the road that you're skiing down, you'd better try.

(10) "Slow Skiing" signs:
- (a) Are safety precautions.
- (b) Are intended for other skiers.
- (c) Can be cross blocked just like gates on a slalom course.

SCORING:

For each answer of (a), award yourself zero points. Answers of (b) get five points each, and answers of (c) get ten points each. Add your answers to all questions together to reach your total score. (If you don't know how to add numbers this large, consider buying a snowboard.)

INTERPRETING YOUR SCORE:

0-35 GREEN CIRCLE:
> You do get credit for having managed to drive a Winnebago up to a ski resort. Now that you've discovered that you won't be able to get it down from the resort until spring, you might as well learn how to ski.

40-65 BLUE SQUARE:
> You're moving in the right direction, but if you want to be a real ski bum you need to quit your day job and immerse yourself in the culture.

70-100 BLACK DIAMOND:
> The snow conditions must be really bad if you're sitting indoors taking quizzes.

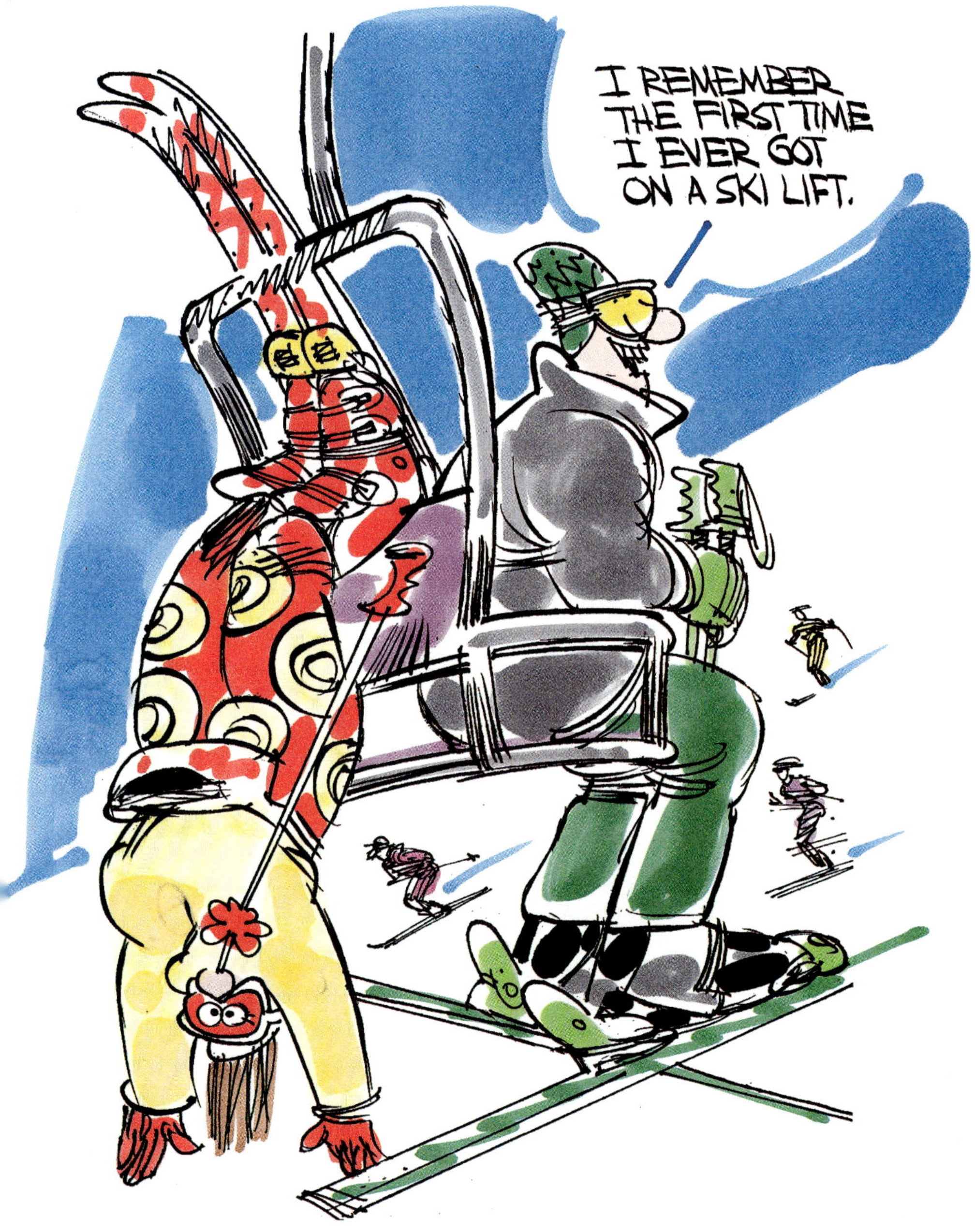
I REMEMBER THE FIRST TIME I EVER GOT ON A SKI LIFT.

Chapter 12:
A Ski Bum's Dictionary

Although inexperienced skiers sometimes speak normal English, the hard core use a language heard nowhere under 7,000 feet. Experts suggest that these linguistic aberrations are due to prolonged oxygen deprivation.

ACL: A piece of GORE-TEX® implanted in the knees of expert skiers.

AIR: Time spent with skis and body completely out of contact with snow.

AIRHEAD: Person who frequently gets big air.

ANKLEBITER: Young skier possessing an appalling ability to snowplow straight down the steepest mogul runs on the mountain.

BRAIN: Not needed by serious skiers. "No brain, no pain."

CAT TRACK: A road so narrow and slick that it can only be negotiated successfully by a skier possessing the same size, agility, and number of lives as a cat.

CHUTE: A steep narrow strip of snow leading down a cliff face. Also, the mildest of the expletives uttered by skiers who catch edges while skiing them.

DAFFY: An aerial maneuver in which a skier does a split in mid-air. Also the name of a duck with roughly the same intelligence level as skiers who execute this maneuver.

DUAL SLALOM: The only ski race format in which you have the option of crashing into your opponent if you think you're in danger of losing.

FALL LINE: The line skiers follow when falling downhill. Not to be confused with the lift line, which is the line skiers follow while waiting to head uphill.

GARAGE SALE: A crash in which ski equipment is detached from the skier and spread out over several hundred yards of the ski slope. Also a place to sell your equipment after you've suffered one to many garage sale wipeouts.

GATES: Tall, slender poles placed on a racecourse to force skiers to make turns. Ski school classes serve as excellent human gates for non-racers.

GROOMING: A process by which most resorts spend millions of dollars to flatten out all available powder snow in order to enable intermediates to crash on the steepest parts of the mountain.

HELICOPTER: A stunt involving rotating in a 360 degree circle in mid-air. Also a vehicle used to rescue skiers who've crashed in otherwise inaccessible terrain after performing such stunts.

INVERTED AERIAL: Any trick which involves the skier hanging upside down in mid-air. Not to be confused with the PERVERTED AERIAL, a maneuver accomplished by two skiers after the lifts close in a bed with new boxsprings.

MOEBIUS FLIP: An inverted aerial involving a simultaneous twist and flip. Certain historical linguists trace this as a possible etymology for the phrase "flipped out."

MOGUL: A large, round bump consisting either of snow or of a fallen male skier with a large beer gut wearing a white powder suit. The only way to tell the difference is that snow can't belch.

PACKED POWDER: A granola bar crushed to a fine powder inside a hip pack by several massive wipeouts.

SKI SWAP: A place where you can sell ski pants which don't fit in order to buy skis you won't like.

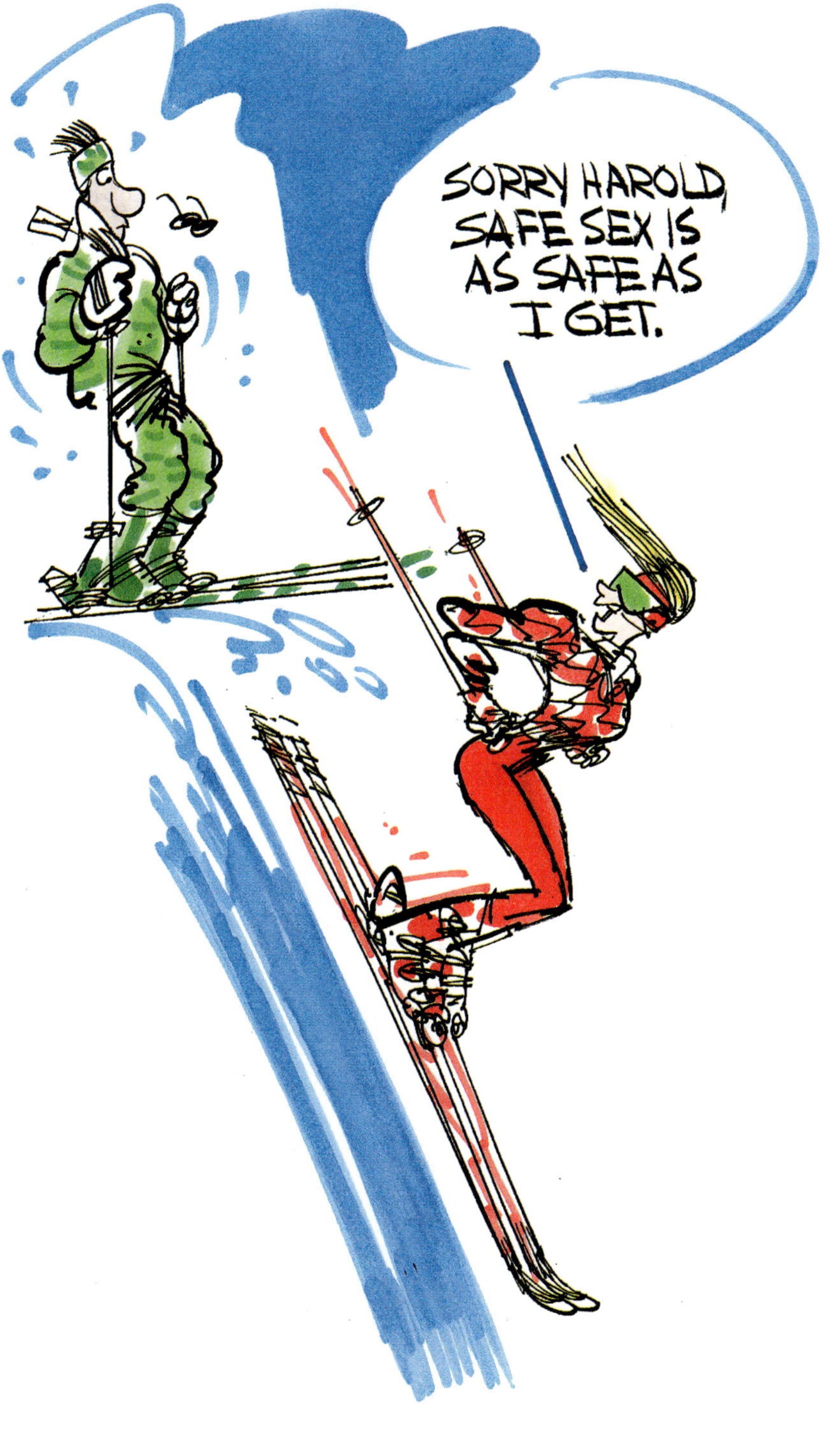
SORRY HAROLD, SAFE SEX IS AS SAFE AS I GET.

SNOWBOARD: A high-technology device designed to enable Californians to negotiate ski slopes safely. Unfortunately, no similar device exists to help them negotiate the roads leading up to ski resorts.

SNOWPLOW: A method of skiing downhill by keeping the tips of the skis together and the tails apart and using the inside edges of both skis to control speed. Also a grooming device that drives up the cat track you're snowplowing down.

SURFACE LIFT: A device used to increase glove sales at small resorts.

TREE HOLES: Either (1) natural indentations in snow surrounding trees into which unwary skiers occasionally crash or (2) unnatural indentations in trees surrounded by snow caused by unwary skiers crashing.

TREE SKIING: What most skiers actually do when they're trying to ski between the trees.

WHITEOUT: A snowstorm so intense that you can see nothing but white snow while skiing, resulting in a sensation of extreme vertigo. So called because much the same sensation can be acheived by painting the inside of your goggles with whiteout and then going for a roller coaster ride in North Dakota in mid-winter.

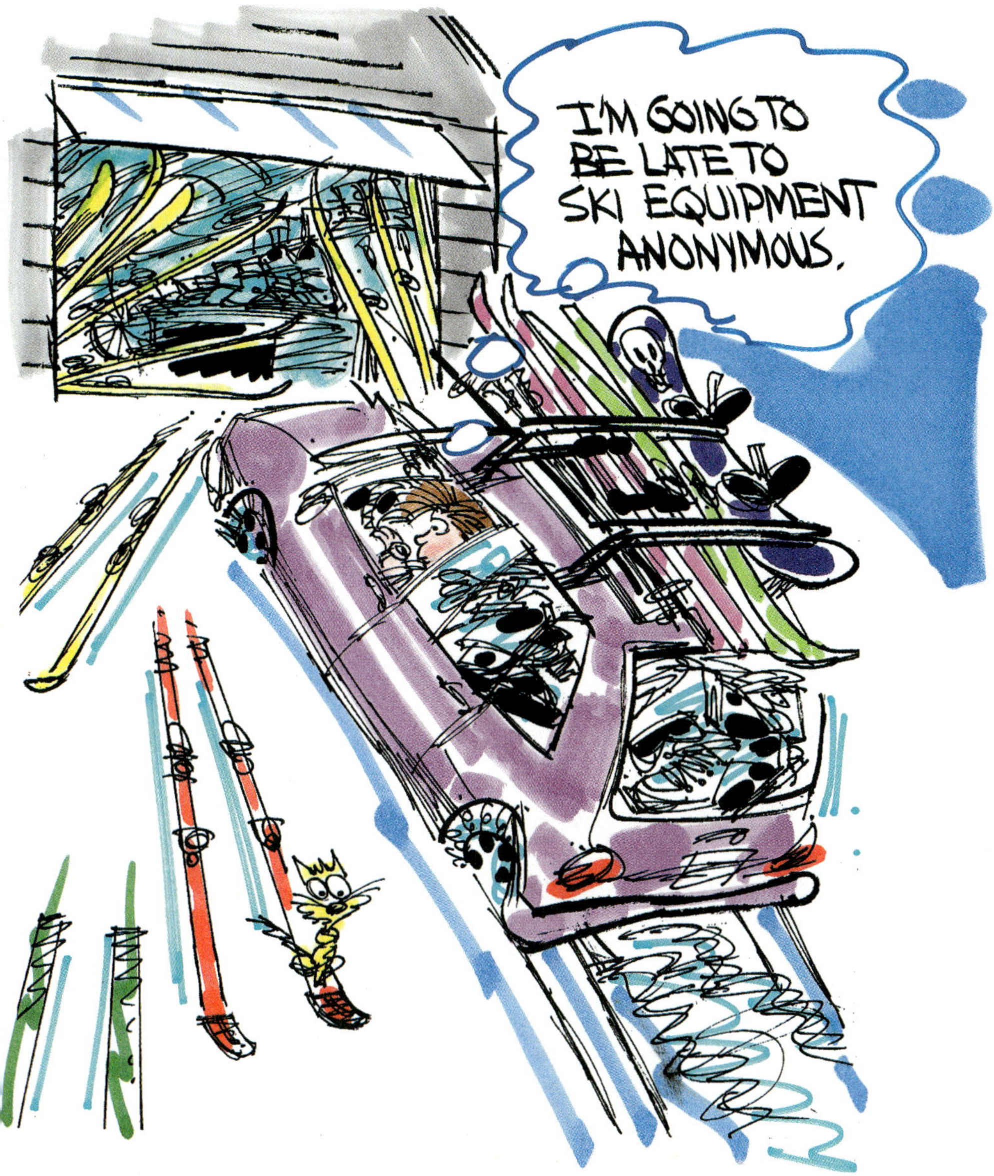
I'M GOING TO BE LATE TO SKI EQUIPMENT ANONYMOUS.